Beneath the Bamboo: A Vietnam War Story

C0-GEH-963

by

Stan Taylor

-Copyright 2016 by Stan Taylor-

License Notes

This eBook is licensed for your personal enjoyment only. This eBook may not be re-sold or given away to other people. If you would like to share this book with another person, please purchase an additional copy for each recipient. Thank you for respecting the hard work of this author.

Editor's Note

This is a first-hand account of a true American soldier's story, written in his own hand, and then edited *only* for grammar and published by his son. The almost half-a-century old memories contained within come directly from an author who would try not to think about war, rarely talked about it, and never wrote about it. Until now. Therefore, it must be understood that this book, in no way, shape, or form, will read like an exact, to-the-letter Vietnam War story. The reason is because the memories contained within are from a real senior citizen who was involved in the conflict who *completely* separated himself from it when he came back home.

Unlike a lot of books available on the Vietnam war, this was *not* written by someone who has been reading war stories since the war happened, a historian, or someone still mentally immersed in their own past in Vietnam who has kept every last detail in their minds present. No, this is a memoir based on the memories of a late teen caught up in one moment in time who just did his job, got out of there, and hasn't looked back until recently. So, please, respect the story and the patriotism of the author, and take all that was said into consideration when reading it. He remembered what he could, and that's all we can ask for. Due to that, we now have a story based on his past that we can all share, and perhaps even learn from.

Dedication

Published for my father, the bravest man I've ever known.

"Oh, the tears I have shed over the years.
Remembering the fallen soldiers and their fears.
Time ran out for oh so many in this twisted land.
But for their country, these soldiers made their last stand.
God, give me the strength to write this story.
Many sacrificed their lives.
They're the ones who deserve the glory."

Table of Contents:

The Angels On My Shoulders

Farewell: The Bamboo Bye-Bye

Are We Done Yet?

Life Lessons

May 12th, 1968

It was Mother's Day, a day of celebration for most. But for us, it soon became the world's biggest nightmare. When we first arrived in Dong Ha, the northern part of southern Vietnam at seven a.m. on a low-key airstrip, we were in awe of the serenity of the spacious scenery. You see, after spending seven months in the dense, steamy, mosquito-infested jungles of this God-forsaken land, this was as close to paradise as we were going to get. It's funny, but it wasn't until this day that I truly stopped trusting my vision. I found out first hand that liking the way something looks gives no guarantee that it won't turn around and bite you in the ass.

The morning had started off simple enough. We all landed in three Chinooks, our personal transport helicopters of the day, and then walked carefully on the outskirts of the city. It was easy to disregard the 105-degree temperature since it felt like an arctic blizzard compared to the sweltering 115-degree jungle heat *we* were accustomed to.

After three hours of monotonous walking, we all noticed four highly stylized sand dunes, each about the size of a four-story building. Noticing that we were all mesmerized by the unusual shape of these creations, our company commander quickly snapped us out of our trances. He ordered our 240 man troop to spread out, but not until he had four point men to lead the way.

A point man's job is to venture out in front of his company by 25-100 yards to watch out for the enemy.

Since I did this for three months when I arrived, I said I would take the right flank. Three greenhorns, or new recruits to a civilian's ears, volunteered for the three positions on the left. We walked out slowly, feeling somewhat safe in this vast emptiness. It truly seemed deserted, and you could have heard a pin drop from a mile away. Just then, a mere 50-75 yards away from the dunes, the most horrific form of hell came our way.

An entire battalion of North Vietnamese soldiers hit us with so much firepower that we didn't stand a chance. They had an entire battalion, which consists of four companies, and our numbers were only a fourth of that. We were outgunned, and it showed. It was almost surreal, like what was happening was only a dream, and amazingly enough that is what kept me calm in the face of the storm.

I watched two point men take a 50-caliber machine gun bullet to the head, and watched the third being grabbed and taken behind enemy lines. Two of the enemy soldiers, which we often referred to as gooks, quickly came after me. As I quickly mowed them down with my automatic rifle, I crawled backwards away from the enemy gunfire, using my helmet to push sand in front of me as I went, which made it possible to look behind me. But as I looked back, I realized that my safety net was no longer safe. I saw my entire company falling like dominoes. Medics were running left and right, risking their lives to help others with bravery that even the most amazing soldier couldn't hope to match.

Some of the events I witnessed during that moment were beyond comprehension. I watched a young, courageous black medic take what looked like an 81-

millimeter round to his head, and his whole body instantly turned to smoke. Young nineteen and twenty year old kids were crying like children, but fighting like someone had raped their sisters. So many things were going through my head at that moment, and in one single heartbeat I was overwhelmed with a flashback of my entire life. This is *my* story, from point A to B, of my life and times in the midst of hell on Earth.

Origins

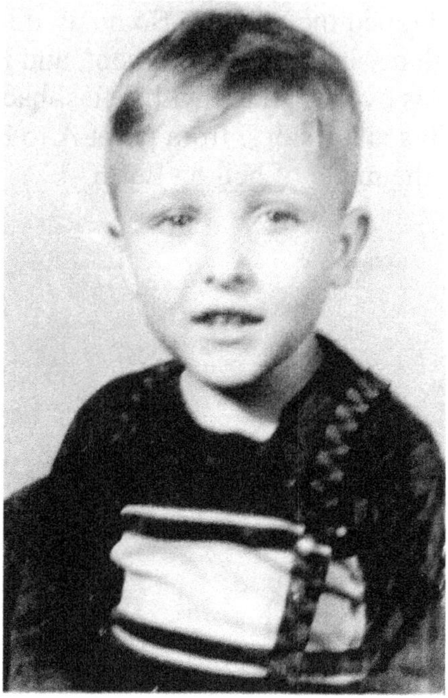

You know, life is funny in the fact that the more complex something is, the more interesting it becomes. But complexity isn't always easy to spot. Sometimes even the most common looking tree off in the distance can become a lot more fascinating the closer you get to the trunk that helped define it.

Truth be told, my story is no different. Talking about the trials and tribulations of wartime is actually a very common thing, but a lifetime of war stories isn't going to convey everything, is it? *Every* story has an origin point that can help shape it into something that gives it a lot more meaning to both ourselves and the world around us.

What I learned more than anything is that *how* a person handles themselves throughout their life, especially during life or death circumstances, has been and always will be a direct reflection of what they experienced as they grew up. I never really understood that concept until now. Who I was and how I was brought up are the reasons I became the type of soldier that no one in my unit could fully understand. But yet, for those very same reasons, I was someone they seemed to admire. I always knew I was different physically, but I never really knew how different I was mentally until my life flashed before my eyes during that one chaotic moment in time.

It all started at the age of two, during the post-WWII era when things would seemingly be better. As I quickly found out, just because one problem is fixed doesn't mean everyone's will be. Although divorces were exceedingly rare during that time, my parents still did it, and my mom and I were left without much hope. Times were tough, but a few years later I was told that she met someone else and was going to marry him. Even though I'm a little fuzzy with those kinds of archaic memories, I *do* recall being extremely happy for us since we would finally be taken care of.

The glimmer of hope she must have seen in my youthful eyes must have looked like heaven sprinkled with the radiance of the icy blue sky on a cloudless summer day. But that look wouldn't last. It couldn't, because what followed was the beginning of fear and discipline that no child should *ever* have to go through. However, there's always a silver lining to every cloud. What was about to enter my life transformed from fear into admiration, and my experiences with this new addition to our family, quite honestly, helped to save my life.

Overall, the beginning years were the worst. When I first met my stepfather, he seemed extremely cold, and quite bitter towards the world in general, like someone had constantly been peeing on his parade. He was built like a bulldog, with a rabid-like attitude and the disposition of a grizzly bear that just had her cubs stolen. Although his anger was usually in control, and my mother sincerely loved him, I could see in her eyes every day that she was *always* going to be scared of the unknown.

I lived in fear my entire childhood due to this, like I was always carefully walking on the eggshells of life, trying not to break them. But the older I got, the more I realized that he was simply a direct reflection of his own tortuous experiences. Like with the tree, *his* emotional trunk was filled with twists and turns that caused his own branches to grow out in numerous, unpredictable directions. You see, he was a lifer in the army. Highly decorated with ribbons and medals, and a long-time POW in Korea, his army buddies simply referred to him as the *baddest ass on the planet.*

Later in life, I learned that he escaped twice from the POW camps. Each time he was caught, they tortured him, but that never stopped him from trying to escape. Most people thought of this man as being nothing more than an indestructible and persistent wall that would never crumble even under the most intense pressure, but he wasn't *all* about being tough. Not really.

Like with most, sometimes actions truly do speak louder than words. From what his friends told me, he masterminded the survival of others. The guards would come around in those tiny, enclosed rooms, take a body count, and give that many bowls of rice to the soldiers who were left living. Many would die of starvation, but my step-dad, whom his friends called Waddie, would prop the dead soldiers up against the walls and toothpick their eyes open so they would be counted as living by the enemy soldiers during chow time. That meant more bowls of rice were put out, giving the ones that were alive more food to eat and a greater chance to survive. Deep within the seemingly cold heart of a man I was always in fear of was *also* a compassionate human being, which is something I didn't really grasp until later in life.

Overall, his experiences were definitely not the greatest. They said he twice picked up a 2x4 board, hit a Korean guard in the head, and stole his motorcycle to get out of the compound, only later to be returned with a severe beating that most wouldn't have survived. I was too young to understand how his resilience and his following misfortune shaped him. Now, however, I *completely* understand. Those in power over him had formed him, but he wasn't about to let anyone have control over him *ever* again, especially a young child. It was at this time that I started to feel his hidden anger coming my direction.

The first time I saw it I was five, sitting at the dinner table and anxiously awaiting the dinner that was being served by my mother. I remember her serving me breaded tomatoes and me loudly proclaiming that I wasn't going to eat them. My stepfather quietly stood up, took all of my food in his hand, and smashed all of it over my tiny face. Needless to say, from there on out I ate everything on my plate.

Another thing I remember is when, in the old days, the television went on the blink and a message would come on that read *Please Stand By.* When this happened, he would make me stand at attention by the TV like some kind of toy soldier until the program we were watching came back on. Sometimes I would be there for two or three hours. He, obviously, was testing me as well as training me to be tough and do what I was told, even if I didn't like it.

Then there's the garage or, as I affectionately called it, the house of pain. He had converted our garage into a beauty shop for my mother, and when I was due for a whipping when I was bad, that was the place I feared the most. After walking three doors down to the old weeping willow tree, he would pull off the two biggest branches he could find. Calmly, and surprisingly enough with no emotion *or* wild rage, he would switch my bare back until I cried or the skin was taken off and I started bleeding.

At the time, I couldn't see him as anything but a monstrous shell of a man. No matter how naughty I may have been or at least what he perceived as being bad, how could a human being do this to another, especially one so young? I just couldn't make sense of it. But, you know, life has a way of protecting you from past pains. I survived. In a way, the discipline and hardship he put me through taught me resilience, fearlessness, and confidence, and I became a survivor because of it. Sometimes bad situations can bring about strength and lessons we sincerely needed to learn. This was one of those times.

He taught me a lot, and throughout the years I have put all of it to good use. However, one thing he taught me stands out more than any other, and it all had to do with equalization. It is what helped to save my butt time and time again, and formed me into a man who always knew he could do anything.

You see, being much smaller than the other boys by leaps and bounds, this is something I sorely needed to learn. He taught me that if you are fighting a person that weighs twenty more pounds than you, you should always pick up a twenty-pound club. In other words, if someone has an unfair advantage, see if a way exists to *make* it fair. The bigger they are, the harder they fall is something he would always say to me, and to this day I know that in my heart to be true. However, what he failed to mention was the fact that the bigger they are, the harder they hit.

Overall, I look back at what he was doing, and it took forever for me to realize it, but he wasn't *just* teaching me to be strong and without fear so that I could excel in life. He was also teaching me to be a soldier. While part of me was always resentful because of it, later in life I knew fully well that *what* my stepfather was preparing me for was the unknown because he always wanted me to be safe.

All of his teachings, quite frankly, helped to save my life, and even though these gifts were given in a rather twisted way, I know he wouldn't have tried to make me strong if he didn't care. Yet, at the same time, his lessons *probably* made me too eager to take risks that I shouldn't have taken in order to prove that I had what it took to be strong. It was, truly, a double-edged sword, and one I will *always* know exists within me after my experiences in Vietnam.

<u>*Changes*</u>

After being trained as a child in ways that would make most run for the hills, never to be heard from again, I entered the always-uncertain years of early adolescence. I admit, most of my years in high school are nothing but a series of colorful but unimaginative blurs. More than likely I purposefully blocked them out.

As expected, I never really felt like I fit in, always feeling like a true outsider. I would often walk down the halls, looking up at everyone, and them looking down at me like some kind of 1960's leper. Fitting in never seemed like an easy option.

Academically, I was not a studious student, and had to work really hard just to make a C in any course I attempted to take, with a really strong emphasis on the word *attempted.* Being shy didn't help either, nor did being five foot and eighty-three pounds my freshman year, which kind of takes the wind out of your sails in the popularity department. Dating, of course, was a joke. I took out two or three girls tops, but I always felt like their train of thought led them to the question of: "Why am I going out with this little kid?"

It was so bad that I remember playing flag football in Spring gym class, and would beg the coach to let me have my shirt on at all times because back then they would play shirts and skins. I didn't want the other kids to see how truly little I was, and I *definitely* didn't want them to see all the welts on my back from my stepfather.

However, as dismal as things may have seemed, it wasn't long before a beacon of hope appeared in a way that I never envisioned. My luck changed when a couple of friends told me to go out for wrestling, thinking it would boost my confidence. Although I hesitated at first, I thought that if I did that it would be less time I would have to spend at home. It was a win-win situation, so why not?

Surprisingly enough, regardless of my small size they welcomed me with open arms. I had the best coach *ever,* supporting every move I made and, with his guidance, I learned to truly enjoy the world of athletics. This is around the time I finally started to see my stepfather shine. Not only did he support my decision to become a wrestler, but when I was good enough to make the varsity squad, both he and my mother were at every single match.

Things also started to get better in my personal life since I made a lot of new friends. I even met a girl from another high school and we started dating. It was great, to say the least. I never knew that the opposite sex could be so much fun to talk to. We ended up going to my prom, and I was as proud as a peacock that the opposite sex would even look in my direction, much less agree to escort me to such a public event. I found out later in life that she ended up marrying a great guy, and they have children and grandchildren now. It's always a great feeling when you find out that someone who had such an impact on your life in the past turned out so well.

Overall, the rest of my high school term was a *lot* better than how it started, but I was still *truly* happy to get it all over with, graduate, and *finally* start my own life. Or so I thought.

A New Life

After graduation, I had myself convinced that I could easily get a job in one of our factories. At this time jobs were rather plentiful, and I was full of piss and vinegar, with a confident fire that spoke to me every day telling me that I could do anything. In fantasy-land, that would definitely fly. But this is real life, when life likes to treat people like they're a bunch of ants beneath a six-year old with a magnifying glass on a bright summer day.

It's funny, really, and I can't help but laugh about it, but just when you feel like you're on top of the world, life pokes its head out of the clouds and says, "I don't think so." In a way, it's probably good that this happens, because it's nature's way of teaching you humility.

So there I was, a young, cocky know-it-all, thinking he could easily get whatever he wanted. What's with us guys and delusions of grandeur, anyway? Needless to say, failure quickly set in. Although I went to all of the factories within the area, and my friends had no trouble getting on, I was rejected non-stop because of my size. Oh, and I was told that point blank, too. Back in the sixties, equal opportunity laws weren't exactly prevalent, that's for sure.

I then learned that a test was being given in order to work for the Post Office. Our local mailman always seemed to be happy and personable when I was growing up, so I thought, hey, why not? So the day finally arrived, with me being nothing but a bundle of late teen angst, feeling as if this was my last shot at employment before practicing the phrase, "Do you want fries with that?"

While anxiously awaiting the piece of paper that could easily determine my future, they informed the twenty-four of us that only three would be hired, and it would be the top three scorers. After the test was over with and I had a week wait, I found out I was fourth on the exam, so I was, of course, devastated beyond belief.

However, three days later the Post Office personnel called and said I went to number one since the others decided to take factory jobs. At that time, the pay, benefits, and job security for that kind of work was actually better, if you can believe that. But it didn't matter to me, because I felt like I was on top of the world. Finally feeling like a true adult, I was able to move out of my parent's house and get an apartment with three other friends. But, like always, just when I felt like I was on the top of the mountain, something happened that made me feel trapped beneath it.

My world was soon turned upside-down one fateful day as I was substituting a mail route. I was kind of excited that day more than most because I was actually going to be carrying mail on the route that my parents lived on. As I was casing the mail, I noticed a letter addressed to me from the selective service office, without a forwarding address since I hadn't had a chance to change my address yet.

Are you kidding me? Great. I was delivering my *own* draft notice. My life had skyrocketed in the last couple of years, but once again my whole world was tumbling down. It wasn't just due to the job either. First of all, my step-dad had finally started to soften up a bit. In the last couple of years he was literally spoiling me, to be honest with you. He had bought me quite a few used cars. A white 56 Ford, a 3-speed 57 convertible Ford which was black and had red interior, and my favorite, which was a 56 Chevy, turquoise in color with baby moons on the wheels. To top it off, he also bought me a little Honda motorcycle.

I never knew the reason for his out-of-the-blue generosity, but I'm assuming this was his way to apologize for all the pain he put me through as a child. Whatever the case, as a newly graduated young man who never really had much before that time, I was very appreciative of his gestures.

However, I don't really think it was the new job *or* the new gifts that made me dread what I had just received. It was because of my new girlfriend. She was incredible. When I first saw her, I just felt compelled to walk up to her and say hello. I'm actually surprised I did. I think on a normal day I would've been so intimidated by her that I would've walked the other direction.

She was, after all, a true goddess in every sense of the word. Hands down, she was the most beautiful girl I had ever laid eyes on. Slender, long blonde hair, big doe eyes that could have made anyone melt, soft, smooth, glowing skin, and a face that had such perfect bone structure and was so blemish-free that she looked like she belonged on a runway, modeling the latest clothes for all to see.

I was totally shocked when she showed interest in me. Not only due to her own looks, but also because prior to me she had been going with a guy that looked like he walked right out of GQ magazine. He was also with a professional skating group called Holiday on Ice. A good-looking, tall professional skater, and she dropped him for *me*. To this day, I have never figured *that one* out.

Whatever the case, I finally had my dream girl, but *now* I risked losing her. It was a tough day when I received my draft notice, and she was one of the primary reasons for that. I truly did not want to go. However, no matter how much I knew I risked leaving behind, I knew I couldn't risk my freedom, so I had to honor the draft.

Weeks later I went to St. Louis to take my physical. Truthfully, since there was a war going on in Vietnam, I was actually hoping I would flunk it. I actually thought I would. After all, I was a runt compared to all of these other young men. As I stood in line, watching what seemed like perfectly healthy Captain America types being declared 4-f, unfit for duty, I thought I would instantly be declined. I went through the myriad number of tests, even slouching to make myself seem even smaller than I already was. But then all of my hopes and dreams were shot as the two doctors at the end of the line said that I was perfect for the army. *Holy crap, you're in trouble America!* is the only thing that I could think of when the cushy carpet of my now-normal life was pulled out from under me.

I was informed that I had six weeks before I had to report to duty, and would be starting my training in Fort Leonardwood, Missouri. Things were worked out with the Post Office, and I found out my job would be secure and my seniority would continue when I was away. So I worked and I partied, but most of all I spent every second that I could with my girlfriend, knowing that these could be the last moments I had with her on Earth.

Time went by *so* fast. Strangely enough, even though I knew the future was going to be tough, I was confident enough to the point where I actually felt prepared. I mean, I grew up with the military. *How tough could it be?*

The morning finally arrived at a ridiculously early 3 a.m., and it was time to depart for service. Two busloads of nineteen and twenty year olds were all facing the unknown, but I knew. Boy did I *ever* know. I had known my entire life.

As we arrived at Leonardwood and the buses pulled up to their designated stops, I could see four drill sergeants patiently waiting for our arrival. Appearances, as always, can be quite deceiving, because once the doors opened we were instantly transported to another world. They all started screaming at us, barking orders with spit flying out of their mouths left and right without a care in the world, and repeatedly calling each of us derogatory names in the process.

After exiting the buses we quickly stood in formation, and I found myself looking at some pretty hardcore sergeants. Each and every one of them could have easily snapped us like a twig. They had everyone shaking in their boots, but for some reason neither their appearance nor this kind of treatment seemed to faze me.

Then we quickly marched to our barracks, or housing units to the civilians. I felt myself getting hyped up as I saw some beautiful red brick buildings, thinking this wasn't going to be so bad after all. But oh no, they marched us *right past them* and into some oversized, round tin cans that looked like giant storage tanks. They called these Quonset huts. Sadly enough, this was going to be where we lived for the duration of our basic training.

As the doors opened, I spied fifteen bunk beds on each side of the room, thirty to a building. This would seem perfectly normal if I was in a prison in some remote third world country, but it's definitely not what I imagined they'd provide for *us*.

After quickly putting our stuff away, the first thing we did was march to the supply area in order to be fitted for a uniform. Then they made us run, and I do mean run, to the mess hall. The food was horrible, making my old grade-school cafeteria food seem like something a five-star chef would serve in comparison, but we were told to eat everything on our plate or we would be doing push-ups all night. Then we made two more formations, during which we were informed repeatedly that all of the rules we were given would be heavily enforced. If they weren't we *would* suffer the consequences.

The following morning we were awakened at 4 a.m. with four drill sergeants flipping our mattress so we would all end up on the floor, which didn't exactly feel pleasant since they were made out of unpadded concrete. Formation after formation, harassment to the highest level, and physical fitness that only the strong could survive. I suppose it could have been worse for me, especially if I had been overweight. The instructors loved to harass the overweight, and the name-calling aimed their direction was atrocious. This kind of treatment wasn't for the timid, to say the least.

Meal-time was especially interesting, and the more time went on, the more you learned what you needed to do. I learned to eat my meals in two to three minutes. The drill sergeants would walk up and down the long tables, and if you didn't eat in five minutes they would kick your tray of food on the floor.

Even worse, after several weeks of learning how to do military functions and having our self-esteem whittled down to nothing, we had to do something that would knock us down *another* few pegs. Sgt. Washington, a physical specimen unlike any I had ever seen, was the prime instigator. As for the man himself, describing him at that time would have taken me out of my normal comfort zone. He was, after all, unlike *anyone* I knew prior to that point in my life. Besides, we had very few black people in the town I was raised in and, when I did see them, they certainly didn't look like *him*. He was a towering vision that made me seem like I should be wearing diapers in comparison. Tall was an understatement since he was around six foot four. Coal black, with biceps as big as my head, sporting wide shoulders and a narrow waist he was, overall, built like the Empire State Building.

He was always testing people, too, and this day was no different. Forty of us were instructed to form a circle and count one to forty, depending on where we stood. The instructors would then call two numbers and then those people would have to fight one another via bungee fighting. A bungee, back then at least, was a seven-foot pole that was padded on both ends. While wearing a protective helmet, the object of the game was to, quite simply, knock the other person down.

Sgt. Washington called my number five times, and I could see the smirk on his face every time. On one hand he looked amazed that someone so small could win every battle, but on the other hand that smile indicated that he knew I was getting cocky and it was high time he did something about it.

So the last time I was up Chuck's number was also called. Chuck was a reservist who had to take basic training, and was a big boy at that. He was six foot five and 270 pounds. *What did Chuck do for a living*? He was a defensive lineman for the San Diego Chargers. My odds weren't good, but I *had* to show Sarge that I had no fear. Something within me was compelling me to be strong and succeed. *Gee, thanks Dad.*

I quickly made my move and charged Chuck, hitting him with everything I had. My bungee must have hit him ten times, but he didn't even flinch. He then hit me so hard I thought the St. Louis arch fell on me. *Oh my God. Now that hurt.*

Like the idiot I am I got up and hit him again, after which he just poetically smiled, as if I was nothing more than a gnat that was flying too close to his face. Then he hit me *again*, and I casually rolled outside the circle like some kind of tumbleweed flying through a deserted ghost town in the Old West.

As I looked up, there was Sgt. Washington standing over me. Smiling with those piano-like ivories of his, he looked me straight in the eyes and said, “Good job.” I didn’t win the battle, but I won the mental war by not giving up in the face of the greater odds that were against me.

Overall, we learned quite a bit in basic, but it wasn’t without an occasional mishap. Cleaning my weapon was simple enough but, one day, while disassembling my 45, my finger slipped off the recoil spring and it hit me in the eye. I was left with one blue eye and one brown since that one was hemorrhaging. I was taken out of that company and put in the hospital, but recovered in two weeks and went back to full duty. The only problem is that I had to start all over again, but at least I got to go back to my all-too-familiar sergeants.

They were *truly* something else. I remember when I had one week to go before being done with basic, and the drill sergeants said if our barracks passed inspection the next day we could all go into town if we wanted to for the weekend. You have never seen thirty guys work so hard. We had that place spotless. Not a speck of dust anywhere, and the floors shined like a brand new penny. We were all standing tall when the sergeants came in, completely confident with our work. As soon as they marched inside they immediately started in on how disgusting they thought it looked. Of course they said that. It was their job to make sure we thought nothing was ever good enough.

Our fate was finally sealed when one of them went outside and brought in a twelve-foot ladder and a screwdriver. He went right under the air duct, unscrewed the metal grate, and then proceeded to put a white glove on. After reaching inside, he pulled out his hand to reveal the glove being turned jet-black. We had just been screwed. They knew what they were doing. We never had a chance to leave the complex before our term was over with. Maybe they were teaching us the fine art of being disappointed. *Who knows*?

It didn't matter, really, because a week later my term was finally over with. Let me tell you, it was *great* to finally graduate. Both my mom and my step-dad attended the ceremony, and it was really great to see them again. In addition, since it was my last day I had finally received my orders on where I was headed to after basic, which was advanced infantry training in Fort Polk, Louisiana. *Little Vietnam, here I come*.

However, before that happened, we were given a brief break. I ***finally*** had a chance to spend time with my honey. It's funny, really, but my friends just couldn't see what she saw in me. I think that must have been the jealousy talking. They knew what I saw in her, though. When she held my hand everywhere we walked and put her arm in mine *everyone* knew how I felt about her. Why? Because they could see my heart beating strongly right through my shirt.

It was a given since she treated me like I was the only one on Earth. Not only that, but she quickly figured out how to be in the good graces of my parents. She would help my mom cook, and would try to soften up my step dad. Overall, they both loved her to pieces.

Unfortunately for me, things didn't easily flow the other direction. When I was introduced to her parents I didn't seem to have the same effect. They were very religious, did not like her dating me, and were *still* set on her marrying Mr. GQ. It wasn't until later in life that they welcomed me into their lives with open arms, but it definitely took a while.

Regardless of that fact, during the two weeks I had my break I cherished every moment I was alone with her. However, like with anything in life, all good things must eventually come to an end. Time flew by with but a blink, we said our goodbyes, and before I knew it I was on the bus to Little Vietnam.

It was a sad moment, but yet at the same time one that had much more clarity than the time before. After all, my new destination was talked about in detail so I *knew* what to expect.

Fort Polk, Louisiana was, from all that I heard, a nasty assignment. A hot, humid miserable swamp of a place armed with mosquitoes the size of dragonflies, it didn't exactly sound like paradise to the others on the bus that were with me. However, for me, after all of my training, I could only think of one simple phrase. *Bring it on.*

When we finally arrived in the mid morning hours, two drill sergeants were awaiting us. We were shocked when they told us in a *polite* way to form a formation and then we'd be marched to our barracks afterwards. *Wow. No name calling, and no screaming at the top of their lungs? Were my sergeants replaced by pod people like in that science fiction body snatchers movie?* Don't get me wrong, it was great, but after the hell we went through it certainly wasn't something we were used to.

However, not everything was better. After marching to our barracks, most of us stood there in amazement. Not in a good way, mind you. The buildings looked like something out of the 1800's, but not in a cool, historic way but, rather, in a condemned building sort of way. They were two or three story tan buildings that looked so old and unkempt that I was quite shocked that they were still standing.

Yet, our horrible accommodations seemed forgivable once we were finally settled in. The primary reason was because we were *casually* told when chow time was and we were asked not to be late. You heard me right. Asked. *What, no marching or running to the mess halls? No threatening punishment? We're on our own? Are you kidding me?*

As the evening progressed and chow was over with that evening, we finally settled in for our first night. We soon learned that every night from this point on was going to be difficult to sleep through since we had no air conditioning of any kind whatsoever. The building inside showed 91 degrees at 8 o'clock at night. *Welcome to little Vietnam*. No wonder they shipped us off to Louisiana. It was to get acclimated to these kinds of temperatures for when they ship us off to the middle of the jungle out in no-mans-land.

Sure, we dealt with it, but it certainly wasn't easy. Due to the intense heat, time seemed to move rather slowly. However, although the next few weeks were tough, they weren't as mentally draining as basic training because we were being treated a *heck* of a lot better.

Don't get me wrong, our minds and our bodies were still used because everything we were taught during this time was a lesson in survival. We had to run five to ten miles quite often, depending on whether or not the sergeant had a date. Hand to hand combat was something we were involved in every single day. Sure, I was on the wrestling team back in high school. But we're talking about lessons on how to kill a man with your bare hands. They certainly didn't teach *that* in gym class.

We were taught a variety of twisted little things, like three different choke holds, crushing an Adams apple, putting seven pounds of pressure on a collar bone to make it break, and even how to heel stomp a head with an extreme amount of aggression. Needless to say, these are things they don't exactly talk about in the modern "*Be all you can be*" commercials for the Army. I really don't think these young kids nowadays truly understand what they're getting themselves into when they purposefully sign up for something like this. This wasn't a video game, this was *real,* and reality can be harsh.

Oh, and up close and personal fighting was only the tip of the iceberg, too. We learned so much in such a short amount of time that it would seem overwhelming to most civilians. For starters, how to disassemble a 45 or an M16 and clean them so they wouldn't jam was especially important. As for one of the more advanced strategic things we learned, we were taught how to read a military map that has nothing but terrain and the elevation of the ground printed on it.

We also learned how to fire a multitude of weapons, including the grenade launcher and how to set up an 81 millimeter. Inner base plate, outer base plate, the tube, how to drop the rounds in the tube, and what to do if there is a dud and it comes out without firing. In addition, we learned how to throw a grenade, how we were supposed to pull the pin, and of course when we were supposed to release our grip.

It didn't stop there. All of us also learned the differences between firing an M60 machine gun and a much larger 50 caliber machine gun. *That was fun*. In addition to gun type differences, Bayonet instruction was *also* a common occurrence, and we learned how to lunge or thrust our arm all the way to our elbow in order to achieve more penetration.

Claymore mines and their appropriate use was also learned, which mainly had to do with the right height to set up the trip flares. We learned how much C-4 to use and where to place the blasting cap. Radio instruction was also stressed, and we learned how to call in air strikes or the artillery units by using a plotting board to call in those strikes at an exact location.

It all seems overwhelming and highly technical as well as physical and, truly, it was. But unbeknownst to most, we weren't just trained in fighting and strategy. We were also taught how to deal with death, how to deal with life, and how to deal with the unknown. It was important to learn how to separate ourselves from civilian life so that we could do our jobs but, at the same time, know how to deal with grief and be human. That was a very important concept that was constantly stressed.

However, the *ultimate* goal in our training was still how to survive in the jungle at all costs while showing no mercy. Even if there isn't one going on, the army *trains you for war*. It's not some kind of vacation or pool party. Don't believe what you hear on TV when the Army stresses learning a new job skill and that's all they focus on. While that may be something you pick up, their ultimate goal is to form you into a fighting machine capable of defending yourself, eliminating the enemy, and defending your country. Learning stuff along the way is just a perk but, honestly, most of the stuff we learned was *not* something we would ever have to use in real life. It was kind of like Algebra.

Whatever the case, having finally learned how to survive even in the harshest of circumstances, we were nearing the end of our training. We had three days to go before graduation, and our biggest test was coming up at midnight, but no one knew what it was. Once twelve-o-clock finally made its presence known to us, they sent our entire unit to the outer parts of the fort. It wasn't just dark, it was without a star in the sky dark. We're talking pitch black.

In front of us was a mile section of woods, and we were told that we had to walk through it and get to the other side without getting caught. If you were caught, you would have to go with whoever touched you and you could *not* resist, or else you risked having to take advanced training all over again. It was like a modern day war game, and I was completely up for it.

I was in the back of the pack, and a friend of mine high tailed behind me. Everyone but he and I started to run. My small but once-powerful ears could hear the voices of guards saying to many of the others, "You are caught." After hearing this, we decided to climb a tree for safety. We waited there, quietly, and after about an hour decided to make our way down and try to walk through the woods. The walk seemed like an eternity. Eventually, we ended up arriving on the road where the bus was, and there were only two others that made it through the forest safe and sound.

The four of us headed to our barracks. We then abruptly woke at 6 a.m. to an abundance of sirens, and were told to go to a certain location for an assembly. Picture this. It was just us four in the audience, and we were about to view what happened the night before. One by one, my fellow soldiers were brought out, most with huge, swollen lips.

It was at that point that the story was told. After each one was caught, they were placed in large drums with a sealed lid. Continuous pounding on the lid from their captors made it seem like an eternity for each soldier. They were then removed from the drum, and laid flat on their backs. A piano wire was stretched across their upper lips within ¼ of an inch, their heads were tilted back, and water was forced down their nose through an eye dropper.

Naturally, they would raise their head, only to have their upper lip cut. All this time they were asked their rank, name, and serial number, which every soldier gave since that is the only information they were supposed to reveal. However, they were *also* asked details about their family and their personal life. Because of the torture every single soldier gave in and talked. I was dumbfounded. In a way, I kind of wish I had been caught because I had been tortured in one way or another all my life. Because of that, I don't believe I would have said one damn word.

Three days later after the incident that gave many of my fellow soldiers a giant wake-up call, the big day finally came. At last, it was finally time for graduation. My parents and girlfriend weren't able to make this one, but that was okay because I was coming home before being deployed.

After all of the parades and the marches in our dress uniforms, we settled down in our barracks while the platoon sergeant handed us our orders. Two of the young men were going to Germany. Lucky bastards. We weren't at war with Germany. At least not *this* decade we weren't. Three were going to Vietnam, assigned to an artillery unit. The rest were going to Vietnam, but assigned to the infantry. My military Occupational Specialty was going to be 11B or, in military slang, 11 Bravo. That meant *straight* to the infantry.

Was I scared? Damn straight. But, for now, I was enthusiastic to be able to go home for a little while for some r & r. After I arrived, my friends were always calling me to go out and party, but I had a beautiful woman waiting on me, and I intended to spend every waking moment that I could with her.

We had talked about it before because of how much we were in love, but marriage was now a necessity for the both of us because she was now carrying my child. When we first talked to my parents they were, as expected, elated. Her parents, on the other hand, were told of the news and they immediately wanted to talk to my parents. Needless to say, things did not go over very well, and they did not want their daughter to marry me. I remember them saying it wouldn't last six months. As a side note, we just had our 47th wedding anniversary, so we can't *always* say our parents are usually right, can we?

You know, I remember that day extremely well. A little *too well*, actually. Her parents stormed out of my parent's house, and my future wife was on the verge of tears after she just finished telling them that she didn't need their blessing. Well, after two days passed a good friend of mine and his wife accompanied my fiancé and I to Michigan City, Indiana. We went straight to a justice of the peace and were married.

After that time, an abundance of unanswered questions overwhelmed me. *Did I make a mistake? Did I rush into this too quickly?* I mean, I'm going to war, so was this a fair thing to do since I might not make it home? Fearful, but on top of the world, the next two weeks went faster than the speed of sound. Each and every day was closer to the day I would enter the unknown.

The last night before departure, we cried together for hours on end. *What will be my final destiny?*

Finally, the day arrived, and it was time to depart. My parents and my new bride bid me farewell, and I knew deep in my heart that this may be the last time I saw my family, and may never get to see our new baby be born.

I left my family far behind, and boarded a bus to St. Louis, and then a flight to Oakland, California. While looking around, I noticed that several young men were on that flight, all dressed in their Army dress clothes. *Are these young men the ones I am going to war with?* I sat there the whole time wondering if they were as nervous and fearful as I was.

After the plane finally landed, we were taken from the airport to a training center and then were told to report at seven the next morning in order to be taken back to the airport. Meanwhile, I made five new friends, and we decided to spend the last stateside evening in Oakland seeing the sights. So we took a cab, and the driver took us to some part of the world that was extremely foreign to all of us. Lots of tents were set up on sidewalks, and every other corner was infested by what we considered undesirables.

As we were walking along the sidewalk, a car with four women pulled up beside us. A lot of the young guys I was with were really showing their immaturity by yelling and whistling. That was to be short-lived, and would soon be followed by gut bursting laughter. The passenger in the driver's seat asked us if one or two of us wanted a ride, but it was in the most baritone voice I've ever heard. Apparently, the car was filled with a bunch of cross-dressers.

Hey, I'm from the middle of a giant cornfield in the Midwest during the 1960s here, so that was something I had never seen before. The laughter from all of us went on for hours after that incident, so apparently they hadn't seen that kind of thing either.

After we all went back to our accommodations after a really fun night, we slept our last peaceful sleep before it was time for the inevitable. Oh how I dreaded to go on that plane ride, and you could tell by the looks on the faces of the other men that they were feeling the same thing. It was a sixteen to eighteen hour ride, all on the same flight. We did stop at Guam to re-fuel, but that was it. The ride was somber, to say the least. Hardly anyone spoke a word. *How many of these young men were going to come home in a body bag? Would I be one of them?*

Finally, the plane touched the ground. I am still amazed at how the pilot landed such a large plane on such a small airstrip. *What was I to embark on when these doors to the plane opened? How safe* **were** *we at this location?*

As the doors slowly opened, we ventured out into this vast, new world. Holy hell, we just stepped into Satan's playground. It was hot. **Damn** hot. You had to struggle just to catch your breath. As I did I looked around and could see army trucks with no tops, all as open as could be. Young men were scurrying about like leaves dancing on the pavement during a gust of wind in the fall. Many were without shirts, only covered up by their fatigues and combat boots.

Most of them had no weapons in their possession, which I thought was extremely odd. I had envisioned all kinds of shooting as soon as I set foot in this primitive country like I had seen on segments from the news, but this didn't even look as bad as basic training.

We had landed at the Bien Hoa airstrip, which I found out was basically like standing in line at Disney World. As we walked by we saw an assortment of army vehicles, one after the next, filled with troops. It was obvious that this was but a pit stop on our destination towards the deeper jungles, and we would soon be in transit once again and easily blend in with the other confused faces in the motorcade.

I felt foolish, as did the other men who were sitting in the back of our new mode of transportation. We were all wearing our dress uniforms, sitting in the back of this truck with heat so unbearable that it would have made the devil sweat. Someone truly didn't have their crap together when it came to this dress code.

Suddenly, and without warning, the convoy took off. We instantly became part of an entourage of twenty trucks, filled to the brim with baby faced kids, looking at their new world in amazement, but with something else that was far too obvious. Every drip of cascading sweat on their face was a direct reflection of what was behind it. Fear.

Everyone knew, especially the drivers, but they tried to keep our focus by explaining to us about our location. As we were riding along, I heard one of the drivers mention that a plane lands every 45 minutes to an hour with new personnel. Great. More buddies to share this foreign sauna with.

We were the equivalent of being stargazed as we saw this newfound alien countryside whiz by us on our long journey. Little Vietnamese children spotted the landscape, often walking down the street completely naked. Some were as young as three and four years old, without a parent in sight. Water buffalo were sporadically seen grazing on a rare patch of grass, which seemed to be in short supply.

The dirt roads, combined with the traction of our vehicles, made our view look like a soot-filled dream that took place in the midst of a dust storm, and it was a dream we weren't allowed to wake up from. All of the Vietnamese civilians, when they were dressed, were almost always dressed the same. They wore drab colored clothing, often extremely soiled and looking like they had worn the same outfit for a decade.

Old Vietnamese women often waved, smiling with teeth that were completely black. I have been told that for some this was caused by chewing what was called betel nut, but for others it was a ritualistic lacquer that older women used to protect their teeth. Whatever the case, it was like Halloween every time one of them smiled.

Their skin was just as harsh. Extremely dry and very weathered, I personally think that their water buffalo had smoother looking skin. They all stood no more than four foot nine to five feet high, and the men weren't much taller at around four foot eleven to five foot four. The younger women put their elders to shame, and it was always difficult to believe what they would turn into. Long, silky black hair, like strands of shiny black diamonds wrapped around silk, skin so smooth it looked like cocoa butter, and a smile with no sign of blackness anywhere, revealing their pearly whites, which would make even the strongest man melt.

As for the old Vietnamese men, they always had us confused whenever they looked at us. We could never tell if they were looking at us with scorn or as their possible saviors. Like the women, they often looked beyond their years, due to the same hard work in the sun that they did like clockwork on a daily basis. The younger men were scarce, probably off fighting the Viet Cong or, worse, joining their ranks and fighting us. If they were around, they looked tired and angry, although every now and then you *would* see one smile, making us feel welcome.

The journey continued, and after we grew accustomed to our view, we quickly became focused on our environment. We had lost track of the army truck in front of us due to the massive amount of dust that was being created, and we were all sweating like a Polar Bear in the Sahara. This was pure misery. *Man it's hot.* I thought Louisiana was a sweatbox, but it didn't even come close to this, and we've only been in the country for a whopping ten minutes.

Just as I felt like I had lost ten pounds of water weight, which I really didn't have to give, I saw a sign that read *Welcome to Long Binh.* Yet again, I'm surprised by what I see. On the outer perimeter I saw many armed soldiers, but casually posed, talking leisurely and smoking cigarettes. Some even had their weapons leaned against sandbags while they played catch with a baseball. Shirts were off, and sweat was pouring off their bodies, but it didn't seem to bother them. They were all laughing and running around like happy little children. *How in the hell did they get used to these temperatures?*

Before I even had a chance to contemplate my own question, our trucks finally rolled inside the gates and then came to an abrupt halt. It seems as though our journey through this mystically foreign foreverland had come to its final destination.

"Stay put and don't get out of the damn truck" were the only words we heard coming from the driver as he quickly left our vehicle.

So we all sat there in this unnerving sweat-box with wheels, waiting on the unknown. We mingled a bit, for some to pass the time and for others to try and brainstorm what our next move would be. Finally, after a long and maybe even intentionally drawn-out wait, a young corporal led us to our new home. For a day, that is. It was a wooden building that we all expected to be as antiquated as everything else in this country, but we were quickly surprised because it had *air conditioning.* Twenty fans, to be exact, all going full speed. *What a relief.*

Sadly, it didn't last long, because we were quickly marched over to the supply tent to get our fatigues. On the way, I noticed that many of the soldiers were not carrying weapons. No helmet, ammo, or backpack, which I thought was quite strange. Maybe Vietnam's not so bad after all.

Once inside, we were given full access to our new wardrobe. Army fatigues, combat boots and a t-shirt. *Where in the hell are my helmet, M16, and grenades?* At this point I began to wonder if the war was over exaggerated. My thought was short-lived, and I quickly woke up from my curious trance as I proceeded to hand over my dress uniform. After they took it and put it in a box with my name attached, I asked when I was going to see it again. The answer was, "When the pearls of hell are over your eyes." *What kind of answer was **that**?*

Afterwards, all of the other new grunts and I were pointed to the mess hall when someone mentioned how hungry we all were. Inside that monstrosity of a tent were tables that looked like they went on for miles. You could see the extremely heavy set cooks sweating profusely over the pots of food they were preparing. *Yum. Fat people sweat.* Perhaps that was their own special seasoning. I'm kidding, of course. Or not. So what was the specialty of the day on our first day? Shit on a shingle, otherwise known as corned beef and gravy on biscuits. We also had carrots and corn and, unfortunately, no dessert.

Dining wasn't what most people would call pleasant. The steam made it unbearable in those closed up tents, adding to the already rising humidity level. We ate in less than three minutes, which was like basic training all over again. The rest of the day was nothing but a blur. It consisted of sitting around attempting to adjust to the new environment and was about as exciting as watching paint dry.

Later that night, around eight o'clock in our temporary accommodations, we all huddled around the fans, trying to make some sense of why it was so late but yet still *so* unbearably hot. Just then, in comes a gentleman who was, surprisingly enough, dressed in civilian clothing. He was middle aged, and didn't quite have the military look one would expect.

He gathered us all together and proceeded to give us a play by play on what was about to go down. We were instructed to make formation every four hours, and if our name was called, we would go with the representative that called us. There were many units that people were being called to go with, and he mentioned them all during our instructions.

We were informed that two units saw the most action. The Big Red One was the first. Supposedly, this was a fantastic unit with really good fighters. Then he looked in all of our eyes and said, "The First Cav division." He looked down as if he saw a ghost. Once he looked back up, he simply stated, "If you go to that unit, may God have mercy on your souls." *What was wrong with that unit? Hell, my stepfather was in the 1st Cav Division.* Almost as if on cue, we all asked why he had such a glum look. He hesitated, sighed loudly, and woefully spoke: "They see it all, and if you're in that unit you will never feel safe."

He told us our first formation was at midnight, so at 11:45 we all gathered around outside to meet our destiny. Suddenly, and quite impersonally, came announcements over a bullhorn of the young men who needed to deploy to their units. A good two hundred names were called, but I was not one of them. So it was back to the barracks for some sleep before the four a.m. formation.

No sooner did I get to sleep, dreaming of the day I would return to my beautiful bride, that I was rudely jerked awake, by a bugle of all things. Again, in formation, with names being called one by one. Yet again, my name was not spoken. It was difficult to get back to sleep with so much adrenaline pumping through my veins as I watched my entire barracks disappear before my very eyes. There were only about ten of us left.

We couldn't sleep, so at six a.m. we jogged down to the breakfast chow line. Scrambled eggs, green in color, reminding me of an all-too-familiar children's book that also involved ham, and bacon that was so filled with fat not once did I feel a crunch while eating it. The orange juice was only a pale reflection of what once was, and was so watered down that it resembled some sort of artificial concoction that only science could produce. *What the hell did they eat in the boondocks? It can't be much worse than this, can it?*

Before I knew it, eight o'clock had arrived, and it was just a handful of us left with what I thought was to be my last formation. Or so I thought. Yep, everyone but me. Again. I made every formation, and no one called my name. Then new recruits started trickling into the building, so I figured it *had* to be my turn to go.

While waiting for the next formation, impatiently I might add, I decided to walk around and explore my surroundings. I couldn't believe my eyes. We had a laundry facility, a movie house, three or four bars, and a bowling alley. Why didn't anyone tell us about these things from the start? That sure would have been a much better way to kill time than huddling inside in front of a bunch of fans.

Noon formation passed, as did the four o'clock and eight p.m. ones. *What the hell is going on?* Again, I was all alone since all of the new recruits were taken. *Have I been forgotten?* I kind of hope so, because the guys that get to stick around for a while get to live like kings with all of this fun stuff to do.

Finally, during the midnight formation on day three my name was called. My last name, that is. As I showed up with the other recruits, I found out that they were looking for someone by the name of Sam. Nope, still not me. Then four a.m. hit and still no call. I was seriously getting sick of this. On the fourth day I thought I'd better ask to see if I was on their roster.

Finally, at the first formation on the fourth day at eight a.m. my name was called. 1st Cavalry Division. *Oh my God.*

Although I was relieved to finally hear my name, I was extremely fearful of my destination. Everyone was talking, saying I didn't want to go there because they were continuously in battle. *Wow, did these guys know how to cheer a person up or what?* An overwhelming amount of fear struck over me, and I honestly thought that I had just been handed a death sentence.

Just as I was being emotionally compromised, with the added help of my fellow bunk mates, a corporal approaches me and tells me that I am in the 2nd of the 5th (2nd battalion, 5th brigade). Next to him was a well built soldier in fatigues who introduced himself as Elvis. The name definitely left me with a question mark over my head since he was a short-haired blonde guy, with no side burns or mutton chops, a seemingly tall five foot ten, and around 170 pounds. *I never did figure out why people called him that.*

Whatever the case, he was the one who was going to take me to my company, which was fine by me since he seemed to be a rather likeable fellow. He was constantly smiling. But his reassuring teeth didn't stop the variety of questions I had constantly roaming through my head at that particular moment. *Why was he not wearing a helmet? Where was his weapon?* As always, I was left with unanswered questions and was quickly moved from one scenario to the next before they could be answered. Today was not going to be an exception, because later that day my adventure into the unknown was *truly* going to begin.

It all started when Elvis took me on a walk about three miles on the outer edge of the compound to a small village. Lying on the ground in the center of the compound was an older Vietnamese man with a long, gray beard, reminding me of an emaciated Charlie Chan. He was dead, with a bullet wound in the middle of his forehead. I was shocked, because no one seemed to care.

Elvis turned to me and said, "He's the village chief. He wouldn't co-operate with Charlie." Charlie, as I found out, was a slang word for the Viet Cong, which was one of the two enemies we'd be facing on this tour. The other being the North Vietnamese army, but we had a tendency to call any of our enemies the same thing.

After my morbid introduction with the recently deceased, we continued walking for what seemed like forever and a day.

"How much farther?" I asked.

"Not far," he said.

After ten more minutes of feeling like a cranky ten year old on a long car trip, we found ourselves looking at a dried up rice paddy, which was apparently our destination. Standing there was a very young Vietnamese boy with an American helmet and an M16 automatic rifle. Seeing him in that helmet made me think of a young boy trying on his dad's hat, with it obviously being way too big for his head. His name was Kit. *Surely* this young child was not in our unit!

Behind him was a pile of supplies, and this is where Elvis picked up his weapon, ammo belt, and his own helmet. Kit handed me the same materials, and then Elvis informed me that I would get the rest of my gear once I met up with the rest of my unit. Twenty or thirty minutes had passed, and I asked why we hadn't left yet.

"We're waiting on the chopper," Elvis replied with a warm, toothy grin.

In the distance, I saw the chopper, or helicopter to a civilian's ears, coming our direction. As it got closer to the ground, I could literally feel the force of the propellers. Slouching over to keep my balance, I boarded along with Elvis and Kit and, I admit, for the first time in a long time I was *really* scared.

We held on for dear life since the doors were left open, and the pilot flew like a bat out of hell. With Elvis on my left and Kit on my right, I felt at least somewhat better being smack dab in the middle. As I looked out, I could see Long Binh escaping my vision and slowly but surely disappearing. Kit kept looking at me in a weird, almost uncomfortable way. I casually mentioned this to Elvis, and he said that he probably hadn't ever seen an American GI the same size as him. He assured me Kit was a super guy, and one that everyone trusted. From what I was told, he was with the South Vietnamese army in Special Forces, which was our ally and, along with us, the direct enemy of both the Viet Cong and the North Vietnamese Army. His mother and father were killed by the Viet Cong, so he volunteered to work with the U.S. forces as an interpreter.

That was all good and everything, but all I could think about at that current moment was whether or not I was going to fall out of that helicopter. I had never been on one before and, with the doors open like that, I was scared shitless. At one point, I decided to test my courage and stretch my neck out a little to see the view. Holy cow, another person was on board besides us three and the pilot. I spied a door gunner on the right side, with a machine gun mounted on a stand. Elvis said there is one on every chopper.

As I strained to see the countryside, I was amazed at the overall beauty of it. Beautiful, green and incredibly dense jungles, followed by open land for miles. Sometimes I would see rice paddies with men and women using their primitive tools and having their husky oxen pull their plows. The terrain was beautiful from the sky, but little did I know that, one day, this was a sight I would truly be sick of.

I asked Elvis where we were going.

"Cav's turf" was his reply. Apparently, we were off to the central highlands of An Khe.

Although we had already established greetings, Kit overheard my questions to Elvis and said, "My name is Kit Carson and we are going to Cong Mountain." To make matters even more confusing he then said, "Purple smoke."

When I looked to see what he was talking about, I saw an abundance of purple smoke shooting upwards, forming a small cloud twenty feet high.

"We're here. That's our landing zone," yelled Elvis in an obvious attempt to counteract the deafening sound of the chopper's blades.

After landing, Kit and I jumped out, Elvis stayed on board, and I was introduced to the GI that threw the smoke grenade. *Okay, I've got it.* Elvis's main job was to shuttle new recruits back and forth. Too bad he's not coming with us.

Welcome to the Jungle

We started walking through a rice paddy, and then into a mysterious jungle like something you would see off of Mutual of Omaha's Wild Kingdom. I followed in amazement as Kit and the other GI walked through this dense greenery like it was an open golf course. After about one hundred yards, there it was. At last. My company.

They were in an open space between the trees, with quite a few soldiers in one location for such a remote area. *Wow. Will you look at these guys?* Their uniforms were old, torn, and brown, and a far cry from the bright green one I had on. Most of them were smoking, with scruff on their faces, and many of them looking like hardened criminals. They all looked at least thirty years old to me, even though there were occasional hints of youth underneath all of that harshness.

Several were pointing and yelling, "Rat."

"Hey Kit, did you bring us a rat?" they all jokingly scoffed. *What were they talking about?* To me a rat is a traitor. Someone who would purposefully pretend they were someone they weren't just to give information to the other side. Surely that's not what they were talking about.

Others were yelling, "Welcome, Cruit." They used extremely short phrases, almost as if they were saving every last breath of energy to keep themselves alive.

"Hey Kit, we'll take him from here," someone yelled.

As I looked up to see my relief, I couldn't help but be visually overwhelmed. Standing in front of me was a hard core looking soldier, close to six foot, and at least 190 pounds. He looked like he could wrestle mountain lions and win.

"Welcome, soldier," he spewed in a southern draw. "My name is Gator, and this is my friend Indy," he quietly remarked. Indy was also tall, but a lean guy with model looking features and coal black curly hair. As I reached out to shake his hand, it felt firm but extremely weathered.

Overall, Gator was a slow talker and fairly quiet most of the time, but when he did talk he definitely got his point across. Whereas Indy talked a million miles an hour, and had a high pitch to his voice. You could instantly sense that they knew their crap, and were both extremely confident of their surroundings.

I sat Indian style on the ground, listening to their every word like I was studying for a quiz that my life depended on. They informed me that I'd be hooching with them and informed me that I needed to listen to everything they said and stay close, but when a firefight broke out that I was supposed to keep my distance. *What did they mean by hooching?*

As I contemplated its meaning, Gator spoke.

"We're going to introduce you to the Old Man and Top. Then we'll take you around to the platoons and you can meet the Louies and the Sergeants that make this company run. You will be assigned to the 2nd platoon with me. Indy is in the 4th platoon, but this unit marches to a different drummer. We stay with the ones we are most comfortable in combat with."

After the speech, we walked about thirty yards, and it seemed as though we were finally in the middle of our little compound. Everyone had their weapon in their hands and their helmet on. Some were sharpening their bayonets on a sand stone. It was at this time that Gator stepped in a bunker and told me to stay put with Indy.

He asked me where I was from and I told him central Illinois.

"Hell, we're neighbors. I live in Indianapolis," he smilingly replied. *Now* I get the connection.

"Gator must be from Florida?" I asked.

"Aw, you're so smart," Indy sarcastically quipped.

A few brief minutes of conversation helped to pass the time, and then a soldier stepped out of the bunker with a communications radio strapped to his back.

Behind him were Gator and a very tall, thin man that reeked of authority. I could see the black sewn Captain's bars on his collar, high up on his six foot three skyscraper-like frame. Compared to me, he seemed larger than life. This was the Captain, affectionately known as the Old Man. As I immediately saluted him he stared, chuckling intensely, as did the others. What I heard then were wise words that helped to give me a sample of what things were going to be like within my company.

"Young man, never salute an officer in this company when you're in the field. We're all brothers here. I'm just the big brother."

Once he was done with my quick scolding, he had his RTO (Radio telephone operator) call the other Louies (Lieutenants) from the different platoons. They were in charge of each platoon and all of them had their own RTO. Here they come, scurrying like little ants. If the Old Man calls, *yesterday* wasn't soon enough.

While I made my introductions, an interesting thing I noticed about these 2nd Lieutenants was that, unlike the assholes that were stateside, these guys seemed really great. My own Lieutenant was no exception. During this time, Gator spoke up and introduced me to Jerry, our platoon leader, with a big, almost sarcastic looking grin on his face. As Jerry, Gator, Indy and I walked back to our platoon, Jerry verbally bowed down to reality and spoke with sincerity as to his real place in the war.

"Don't be fooled by the Lieutenant bars. In our platoon, Sergeant Pete runs the show. Do exactly as he says and you'll be going home in an upright position."

As time went on, even more introductions were made. First, they wanted me to meet Top. He was our top non-commissioned officer, and was pretty much in charge of all the platoons. An E-8 in rank and a seasoned veteran, boy did he ever remind me of my stepfather with his demeanor. He was crusty and pretty hard-core, with an uncertain ethnicity, but I always guessed he was from the Philippines or Hawaii. The Old Man's right hand man, he made and carried out most of the orders and passed them down to the platoon leaders.

When I was introduced to him and extended my hand, he just glared at me with an unnerving look and said, "You look like a rat." *What is this crap with looking like a rat?*

After a brief encounter with this hardened soul of a man, we departed to the 2nd platoon and I was introduced to almost all of my new platoon buddies. They were all completely covered in filth, looking like they were coal miners from the deep hills of West Virginia who just happened to be wearing camouflage. I expected names, of course, but that's not what I got. Everyone around here seemed to use nicknames. Some of the many that I heard were Bird, Rock, Grenade, and a sorry nickname if I ever heard one, Dung. I wonder what the story is behind *that* one.

As I contemplated all of their meanings, Gator firmly spoke up.

"Sgt. Pete, come here. We have a greenhorn."

Just then I witness this tiny little man, not much bigger than me, walk towards me as if he owned Vietnam. When he walked, he was not the small-framed man that civilians on the outside would probably see, but within these jungles it was like he was seven feet tall. He was confidence personified, but as he got closer I could see that it was coated with that of a weary body from a hardened lifetime of being a warrior. Every time he spoke it was with a roughneck tone, and his cold, dark, penetrating eyes watched my every move. I could sense why others gave him so much respect. I felt it. I really did. But at the time I just didn't understand why I was feeling that way.

After he quickly welcomed me, he told me to stay with Gator and Indy, and that I should learn from them. Then he disappeared into the enveloping midst of my fellow GI's. Overall, what he said about learning made me feel like I would truly have a couple of genuinely nice people to count on to guide me through this long path of uncertainty.

However, I would quickly see that learning would never be limited to just a couple of people because, honestly, it was like one big happy family here. Everyone in this platoon knew everyone, really, and it showed. As an example, even though Indy was in the fourth platoon, everyone here in the second was saying hello to him like they had known him their entire lives. This would be a constantly reoccurring theme that would, one day, allow me to see these strangers as my second family. But for now? Now it was just a happy onslaught of new introductions.

Time seemed to be moving as slowly as snails making love while I kept shaking everyone's hands, but the redundancy of these new meets would soon be over with. I was ever-so happy once Gator and Indy told me that a chopper would be landing in a couple of hours with supplies. Apparently, all of my needs would be on that chopper.

"What do you guys eat out here anyway?" I asked. My stomach obviously decided to throw its voice to my lips.

Indy replied with a reassuring, "Don't worry, we eat better than the mess halls. The 1st Cav is the best unit in the world. They take care of their own."

Before my stomach could be appeased, however, I had to make my way to my new home. While walking around with my two new buddies, we eventually came to a small tent. Gator informed me that this was our hooch. All I saw was a big piece of plastic. A hooch was basically two ponchos snapped together and supported with bamboo chutes. Now that's what I call primitive. I looked inside and saw their backpacks and two air mattresses, so I was at least partially happy that we wouldn't be sleeping on the ground.

Once we settled inside, Indy leaned over, and out of a sock that was attached to his backpack he pulled out a small round can.

"Hungry?"

He threw it my way, and I caught it and glanced at the label. *Pound cake.* Then he pulled a metal device out of his pocket and proceeded to show me how to open the can. It was called a P-38, and you worked it like a can opener. Yet again, something they definitely didn't teach us in advanced Infantry training. I put the little pound cake in my mouth, and after three bites it was gone. *Not bad.*

After putting a stop to my incessant belly noises, as well as having a few brief conversations, we started walking the perimeter in order for me to get familiarized with the area. I noticed that there were foxholes dug all around our base camp, and they all looked to be about three foot deep and about four foot around. At least one soldier was in each foxhole at all times. After asking about them, Indy proceeded to tell me that we would all pitch in to dig them whenever they were needed.

As we continued walking, we ended up at the mortar pit. This is where the fourth platoon congregated. I stared in awe of the amazing job the 4th platoon did in digging out the pit. Shells were lying in plain sight, which made me wonder who carried them from one place to the next. Indy handed me one, and it must've weighed twenty pounds, at least. To a little guy like me, it may as well have weighed a ton. While there, he showed me a variety of shells. The explosive ones, the phosphorous ones, and the ones we used solely for illumination. Each soldier in the fourth platoon carried one shell, which made me extremely happy to be in the second. Man, am I ever glad I don't have *that* strapped across my back. Overall, although it seemed like this camp had been set up forever, it wasn't. They had only been at this location for a mere three days, which was actually quite unusual. Usually they didn't stay in one place this long.

Having been shown the mortar pit as well as the rest of the area, I finally gained my bearings and knew the surroundings well. Once I finally felt settled, it instantly became Christmas time for the camp. Choppers! The whole company was smiling, and Gator informed me that this was always the best part of the day. Supplies, chow, and, best of all, mail call.

I watched half the company unload the choppers, and after the crates were opened I saw a ton of supplies, including great big green containers that contained the hot chow. I'm not sure what it was like in other units, but as I found out during my tour we were usually pretty lucky and often had chopper visits twice a day, unless we were in the thick of things and they couldn't get to us. I guess that's the good thing about being part of the Air Cavalry. We had helicopters at our disposal at the drop of a hat.

So there I was, looking at an abundance of new equipment, as eager as ever to start grabbing. But before I could get my mitts on anything, Top walked in to take control. Gator told Top he wanted to get the new guy, yours truly, set up first. *Top nods in approval*. Gator and Indy set me up like they had done this their whole lives. I received a backpack, a roll of toilet paper, a P-38, a small tube of toothpaste, a toothbrush, two ink pens, a pad of paper, malaria pills, a fatigue shirt with a 1st Cav patch on it, ammo clips (We called them magazines), three pairs of socks, a weapons cleaner, an air mattress, a flashlight, and heat tabs. In addition, Gator got me two boxes of C-rations, a poncho, and then proceeds to put mosquito repellent in my bag.

I put the P-38 in my pocket, and picked up the backpack, which I thought was a bit heavy for me, but they assured me that the only real weight was the ammo, and I would need it. In addition, I was also given a fold-up shovel and they assured me I would *definitely* need it, and not just for digging foxholes either. Then they threw me the air mattress and told me to start blowing after we walked back to our hooch.

We all sat around and they told me what I should expect as I huffed and puffed on that air mattress like I was a small child trying to blow up an oversized beach ball. Shortly thereafter, Sgt Pete walked by and yelled, "2nd platoon, let's go."

He did that because after mail call it was chow time. Dogs and Kraut. Food was never in short supply, especially for the guys in the field. We were brought supplies every night with a hot meal most of the time, with only a few exceptions when they couldn't get to us. Even if we didn't manage to have any extras mid-day, we'd almost always have a hot breakfast in the morning and lots of water to fill our canteens.

After we ate, Gator went by the crates and picked up a claymore mine and handed it to me. Apparently I was supposed to put it in my backpack, but back at the hooch I struggled to get the stupid thing in. Indy took out my C-rations and one sock, stuffed the can of c-rations in the sock and then ties it to the top of the backpack. Problem solved, and the claymore finally fit.

While smiling over his ingenuity, Indy tells me that I would be pulling guard with Gator from two to three a.m. Indy never pulls guard because he is always the first they go to in the 4th platoon, so they always need him there to be in charge of the plotting board so he can calculate yardage and the degree to slant the mortar. Needless to say, where the mortar shells go depend on this guy, so he was a prized asset that had to be kept away from the front lines.

It was close to sunset, and once Top went around checking the foxholes to make sure the claymores were set, darkness reared its ugly head and the Old Man told us: "*lights out*." That meant no cigarettes or flashlights. As I soon learned, it was the most dangerous time to be in the jungle.

The three of us headed to our hooch, and I was taught to lay with my M16 right next to me. I was out like a light when all of a sudden Gator nudges me and says, "It's our turn." He then leads me to a specific foxhole to relieve the ones that were there the previous hour. I can't see crap, so he has me hold on to his arm on the way there.

After we arrived, we were there in the hole armed with our weapons and ammo belts and Gator doesn't speak a solitary word. So I look straight ahead and am slowly reminded what darkness is actually supposed to look like. As I place my hands in front of my face, not even a hint of my hands reflect any resemblance of moonlight.

Fifteen minutes go by, and my eyes start to adjust, but I still can't see beyond the claymores that sit past the foxhole.

Thirty minutes pass, and Gator whispers in my ear. "I don't like what I am sensing. I've got to get Indy. Stay right here."

He takes off to the center of our company and is back in less than two minutes.

Five more minutes pass and Gator announces, "Come on, Indy, light them up."

All of a sudden I hear *thup thup thup*, the sound of our 81mm mortar firing sporadically. Five seconds later, the whole sky is lit up like the sun decided to give the moon a break. I blink, and like some kind of eerie silent movie, I had trouble believing that my eyes weren't playing tricks on me.

Holy shit, there's ten to fifteen Charlies running right for us! I started to fire my weapon, but I was already a magazine behind Gator, and the other guys in the foxholes were laying the firepower on thick. In a matter of a few seconds it was all over with. Although the illumination rounds kept going off, I could plainly see that the enemy was all dead, without a second wave in sight.

Gator told me that we would count the bodies in the morning in the daylight hours. We were then relieved of guard duty, and after we got back to the hooch neither Gator nor Indy said a word and they went right to sleep. I, on the other hand, had my eyes wide open for the duration of the night. *The first day in my company and I saw action.*

As the sunrise quickly peeked its head out from the horizon, my weary body, lacking sleep and still pumped with adrenaline, wanted to talk about what just happened. But not one person ever said a word.

Later that morning I walked out to the dead bodies with four other GI's that I had never seen before. I counted eleven dead bodies, and wondered if any of my bullets were responsible. As we walked back towards the camp, I asked what we should do with them.

"Leave them to rot" is what I was told.

The shock of what I heard was disheartening, yes, but it quickly disappeared once two more choppers landed in our zone. I watched a crew load the green containers on one chopper plus the left over supplies as well as the outgoing mail. Another crew unloaded new supplies, more hot goods, and large ten gallon containers of water. It all happened like clockwork. We then stood in line to fill our canteens and eat our meal, which was scrambled eggs and greasy bacon.

Then the announcement came. Top told us we were heading out today, and that we had been on vacation long enough. So we went back to our hooch, undid everything, and put our individualized camp in our backpacks.

An hour later, Top gathered us to tell us that we were going on a search and clear mission. It was just like it sounded. Our job was to search for anything that looked like Viet Cong in the area and clear out the undesirables. It was at this point that I realized we weren't in some pansy-ass group where the upper chain of command stayed behind. Both Top and the Old Man were our backbone, and were always there with us.

Top then told one of our soldiers to take off, and that we would follow him in five to fifteen minutes. Indy told me that was our point man. He was the first to see what was in store for us, and Gator said that anyone who wanted that job was crazy. I'm not sure how it was in the rest of the Army, but in our unit that position was strictly volunteer.

After Sgt. Pete confirmed that everyone had our mosquito repellent, thirty minutes later we trekked into the deep recesses of the jungle. I followed anyone with a machete, which wasn't a whole lot of people since I swear we only had four or five people carrying them in the whole unit. It scared me to think of the possible noise we might be making, no matter how faint, but to get through the really bad stuff we had no choice.

It didn't matter I suppose because, as my troop often told me, "Trust me, *Charlie knows where you are*."

Man, this stuff is thick! As I ventured on, drenched with sweat and having trouble staying focused on the possible danger, the only thing I could think of was that I wanted to survive this unbearable heat.

Two hours later and out of nowhere, we came across a clearing with six huts. One old Vietnamese man, eight women, and around six children were easily within view. Kit runs up to the weathered Old Man, and he sounds like an auctioneer as he speaks a million miles an hour. After fifteen minutes pass, he goes up to our company commander and tells him what he was told. It seems as though the rest of the men are supposedly planting rice in the fields. Our point man then takes off once again. *I've got to talk to that guy sometime. What he does sounds fascinating.*

Then we pass the village and move through the intense jungle for a couple more hours, but the sun was really blaring down on us so we had to stop. It was lunch time anyway, so that gave us a great excuse for a break. The intertwining branches and roots of the jungle were so utterly thick that, even though we were all within a short range of one another, I could still only see about five guys.

After I sat down on the cold, lifeless ground, I started to eat, and I pulled the can out of my sock. On it read *ham and lima beans*. I was told that sometimes we use the heat tabs, but during lunch we have to eat so quickly that we usually eat it cold. Not that it was overly cold anyway, because the intense heat of this forested swampland made the contents nice and warm. Barely palatable, but nice and warm. But hey, that's what water is for, right? I started gulping down my water from my canteen, but was quickly told to just take a few sips because we still had a ways to go.

It seemed like we no sooner sat down and it was time to go. Another hour, then two passed. Then I saw the point man returning to Top and pointing to the left.

After going another 200 yards we come across an area that was previously used by GI's. In a way, this was good because it meant we didn't have to dig near as much because it was already done.

Around this time I kept asking myself what makes the point man tick. He is so full of confidence that I just *had* to talk to him. But not yet. First we had to dig our foxholes, which basically meant trimming them out since they were previously dug. Next, we set up our hooch and set the claymores, and then it was time to eat again as the choppers had already landed.

Again, we got more supplies, mostly ammo as well as a few C-rations. After chowing down, I knew we only had about two to three hours of daylight left, and I wanted to talk to the point man. He was pretty easy to find, really. Although most everyone else had someone to talk to, he was sitting all by himself, writing a letter.

As I walked up to him, I admit that I was a little intimidated. After all, Gator did say he was crazy. But crazy to one person can mean something entirely different to another, so I walked right up to him and sat down beside him. His first words were quite elegant, really.

"What the hell do you want?" he barked.

"I just want to talk. I find you very interesting," I said with an almost juvenile grin.

All of a sudden, the sky opened up and I saw the quickest transformation I had ever seen. He went from being very defensive to being extremely friendly with that one simple phrase. It seems as though all he needed was someone to show him that they cared.

We talked for over an hour, and he was smiling just like he got a new puppy. I guess I was the puppy. It's interesting how people so easily judge a guy by how he presents himself, but as the saying always goes, never judge a book by its cover.

His name was Jim, by the way, but everyone in the company called him Loner. He informed me that everyone in the company has a nickname, and I will too when the time comes. After his few words of wisdom, I decided to ask him if he was scared when he went out every day to pull point.

"Shitless," he replied. Then he said something that really shocked me.

"Let's pull a double point tomorrow, just you and I leading the way. Don't worry, I'll pull it through with the Old Man and Top." Not thinking, which would be a routine happening during my time in the bush, I told him that would be great.

Overall, he told me that he really enjoyed our visit, and as I left him I felt really sad that the others never talk to him. As I walked back to the hooch, I couldn't wait to tell Gator and Indy. After the words rolled out of my mouth, Indy slapped me across the helmet.

"Two or three days and you want to pull point? Are you an idiot?"

"No, I'm just curious," I said. Both Indy and Gator tried their best to persuade me not to go with Loner the next day, but my mind was all set.

Later that night, after pulling guard in the foxhole with Gator with no enemy in sight, I collapsed on my air mattress for a couple of hours. As soon as I fell asleep the new day and the sound of choppers woke me. Sleep was a luxury that I obviously was never going to get. After chow, Sgt. Pete told me to follow him to the company commander and the first Sergeant. I could see them staring me down with the look of *What was he thinking*? written all over their faces.

Here I was, only in the platoon for a few days, and I was being talked to by the Old Man, Top, and Sgt. Pete. It felt good to feel important.

"I hear you want to go with Loner and pull point," the company commander spoke.

"Yes, sir, I do," I confidently announced. Then Top decided to chime in.

"You have no idea. You could be killed the first week over here."

My reply was simple, but elegant.

"That's a long time compared to the first day." *Wow, did I ever get brownie points for* ***that*** *one.*

Top smiles and says, "Get with Loner, go over the details, and for God's sake listen to everything he says." I nod my head, proudly, and out of my mouth came words that I swear were put there by my stepfather.

"I promise you I will. I'm here to learn ***and*** to survive."

After I got with Loner, wow did he *ever* lay it on the line.

"We shoot to kill. We can't ask questions. There is only us. We make our own paths. We do not take trails that have already been used. If we are outnumbered by over two to one, we retreat to our company. Most importantly, we never talk, but communicate through hand signals, eye movement, and body language."

It was highly apparent that the congenial guy that I talked to last night wasn't his only persona. When it had to do with life and saving himself and others, he was strictly business.

Eventually, once we were finally set to go, my heart was playing jump rope with itself, skipping beats at a rapid pace. Even though we would be anywhere from fifty feet to as much as seventy-five yards in front of our company, it would seem like miles out in that dense, dangerous jungle.

When we ventured out, I followed Loner for about fifteen minutes in the dreary, insect-infested forest. Then he motioned for me to go left by about twenty yards. Every once in a while I would catch a glimpse of him right before the jungle consumed him.

We had only walked about an hour when he suddenly froze and then motioned me to come to his side. With his hand over my mouth, he pulled the leaves back, and there was a village of about twenty huts. The village was overrun with about twenty to thirty Viet Cong. They had on their typical black pajamas, and were all carrying their AK-47s (Automatic rifles) with ammo belts around their waists and necks. *I was terrified.*

Loner pointed back towards our company, which was less than a football field behind us. Once we were around 25 yards from the company, Loner made a bird like call to inform them that it was us.

He talked to Top, and it looked like we were going in. 240 of us against 25-30 Cong. Sounds fair to me.

As Loner leads the way, we approach them like tigers on the hunt. The 1st platoon and the 3rd platoon took their stance about thirty yards from our targets. My second platoon was behind them, and the 4th platoon brought up the rear. Everyone was in position.

Top gave the orders to kill them all. A machine gunner who carried an M60 started shooting. Wow was that guy good. He could have won a lot of teddy bears at the state fair, that's for sure. Overall, this little fiasco didn't last but three minutes. The body count was twenty-one.

I was extremely thankful for Loner. In all seriousness, I don't know how I would have handled the situation if I were alone on point. But yet, at the same time, something deep within me cried out for that kind of power. This was far from over. I wanted more, and I was intent on having it.

Over the next several days, we went from one location to another without any confrontation. But what I learned from Loner in times of silence was above and beyond what the typical soldier would learn. The way you walk, what to listen for, and how to focus. He was a soldier's soldier.

My admiration for him was extreme, but my world came crashing down when, a week later, I learned that Loner wasn't pulling point anymore. He had spent his year in this hell hole, and was ready to go home. With only a couple of weeks left, he wanted to be in a safer role. I don't blame him, really. Who wants to risk death if you only have two weeks left before you're back in paradise?

The company commander pulled me to the side, saying the job was mine if I wanted it. Loner told him point blank that I could do it. He also said that I needed to remember that it was voluntary because it was the second most suicidal job we had.

"What's the first?" I asked.

"You don't even want to know," he replied under his breath.

Quickly, we got back to the conversation of pulling point. Since I had the backing of Loner, I felt confident that I could do the job.

"Of course I'll do it," I announced.

It was official, but I couldn't be excited about it until it actually happened. For now we had to set up camp. It would be a while before we were on the prowl again, so I would spend my late afternoons writing letters to my parents and, of course, my beautiful wife. I missed them so much, and even wrote my pregnant inspiration on my helmet. I was still waiting on their return letters, but Gator and Indy informed me that sometimes the letters were three weeks late.

When it was finally time to move again, I was fully aware that it was my first day to lead our company through these jungles. I was truly psyched because it was a lot of responsibility. Sgt. Pete approached me right before we left and asked how I felt about it.

Scared shitless. Yet, at the same time, confident, with a youthful cocky arrogance that made me know that I could do it.

Indy and Gator were telling me not to do anything stupid, and my platoon leader kept saying I didn't have to do this. I got that a lot in my life, so I was used to it. Except for my stepfather, who always pushed me to the limit, most people looked at me and treated me like a child due to my smaller stature. I wasn't about to let people make me out to be a coward.

After hearing that nasty "*Saddle up*" phrase from Top, I was completely focused, but at the same time, life felt a little bit surreal. It was like I was stuck in the middle of a Salvador Dali painting, with melting bamboo all around me instead of clocks.

When it was finally time for me to go, I was fully aware that I would be all alone out there, and that the rest of the platoon would be taking off five minutes after me. Five to fifteen minutes for a point man to lead was pretty common in our group, but considering this was my first solo attempt I'm sure it would feel like an hour. But I couldn't think of that. I *had* to keep my focus.

Before I left, Loner came up to me and gave me a big bear hug in front of everyone. It was a little embarrassing, I admit, but I definitely understood that it was a *just in case* hug that he felt needed to happen.

"Just remember everything I told you and you'll be okay," he remarked. I nodded in agreement, took off, and only turned around once. When I did, everything occurred to me as plain as the nose on my face. *Oh my God, the lives of these men are all in my hands.*

It was time to put on my game face. Avoiding the worn paths, I attempted to quietly and quickly machete my way through the dense jungle the best I could in order to make a brand new path for my group to follow. *What if they can't follow my path? What if I get lost and can't make it back to them?* All of a sudden, I realize that I don't have Loner to rely on. *Stay focused. Stay focused.* Loner was so calm, and nothing seemed to faze him, so I need to keep reminding myself how I need to be. I remember the TV, saluting to the message of ***Stay Tuned***. *Just stay focused. Focused.* After walking an hour and a half, I came across a clearing that I could easily see through all the thick bamboo that always seemed to reach for the clouds. Oh my. Another village. However, unlike the last, this one looked peaceful.

Old ladies were talking by their huts, and a bunch of old men doing what looked like an old fashioned grilling. They had something on an open flame on a rotisserie, but I wasn't close enough to see what it was. The good thing is that I saw no weapons and absolutely no sign of Charlie. It was my first day alone and I found myself a village. Alright!

Extremely excited, I head back to my company. After five to fifteen minutes passed of making my way through the broken branches and sticks I had laid down,

I thought I would have reached them. *Where the hell are they?* When forty minutes passed I was freaking out, thinking they stopped early, got into a gunfight, or couldn't follow my trail.

Then, finally, I see two GI's. I do the little bird call, and they were very elated to see me. But trust me, I was a lot more excited to see *them*.

After telling the Old Man what I saw, we immediately proceeded to the destination. Once we arrived, Kit walked out in front and started talking to the village elders. He said they were friendly, and that no Cong had been there in a year. While we were being given the rundown, I spotted an old man trying to catch a little black and brown dog, which looked to be a pup. The dog was running for its life, and stopped right at the Commander's feet.

Just as the Vietnamese man reached down to pick her up, our Commander picked her up in his arms and snapped, "You go find something else to eat."

Kit then relayed the message, and the old man scornfully walked away. We were then informed by Kit that another dog was what was on their stick that they were roasting. More than likely, that was the pup's mother, father, or one of her brothers or sisters. Here in Vietnam, they don't have pets, and, unfortunately, anything that has legs is food.

The dog just kept licking the Old Man's face. With a smile that defies all odds he said, "You are now mine, and you will protect this company. I shall name you Lifer." He put her down, and from that point on she never hesitated once to follow us everywhere.

As Kit talked to the village chief, we were informed that another American army company had stayed about a hundred yards away the night before. I never got that far, so we all went that direction. Sure enough, a mortar pit was dug, and a bunch of foxholes were in place. At this time Loner came up to me and told me how proud of me he was, which made me feel really good.

Later, we all trimmed out the foxholes, and Gator and Loner told me to bring them my claymore mine. I watched them set it up, and it was obvious that it was something they had done repeatedly during their time here. They were using trip wire to hook it to the detonating device, and the wire went from one mine to the next. They placed the trip wire approximately ten inches off the ground so that Charlie wouldn't be able to crawl under it. Overall, I was in awe of the precision and the rapid pace at which they could set these up.

A little time had passed, and after the helicopters brought us our supplies and chow, once again we felt relaxed. Everyone was slapping me on the back, and I really started to feel like I belonged. Gator and Indy kept persisting that I no longer pull point, but after my first encounter I just couldn't wait for more. Something within me craved excitement, and always made me feel like I had to prove my worth. *Again, gee thanks, Dad.*

Later that night, we were finally secure, and the foxholes were well positioned. I noticed the Old Man, Top, and all the platoon leaders and other Sergeants were all in a huddle. They came around to our hooches and said to pay close attention tonight while on guard duty. Apparently, we had an artillery unit overrun two nights ago only five miles away, and that is where we were headed tomorrow.

Once I laid on my mattress, I was out like a light. Before I knew it, a nudge from Gator woke me out of my somber sleep and, yet again, it was time to pull guard duty. We arrived at our foxhole to relieve those before us, and the guys in the hole said that Lifer, our new pup, had been going from foxhole to foxhole, growling like crazy. Something must be up.

Lifer was a blessing, and gave us all a unique sense of home every time we pet her. She was family now. We trusted her like she trusted us. To an outsider, it might seem kind of odd, but she wasn't just possible protection, but something to remind us of the sanity of the outside world. But above all else, she was the *best* guard dog creation could have produced.

Due to her incessant growling that evening, I asked Gator if we should go get Indy.

"Not yet," he silently rebutted.

Dang it. It was so damn dark. No moon. No stars. Nothing. Everyone was on edge, and you could just sense it because of Lifer. Gator reached over to pet her, and her hair was standing straight up on her back.

"That's it. I'm getting Indy and the 4th platoon out of bed," he quietly announced.

He no sooner jumped back in the foxhole when all hell broke loose. Three Charlies hit the trip wire and they all detonated. They were hit full force from the blast of the small, pellet-like shrapnel, and with that one flash we could see many more coming our way. *Oh my God. Wake up, company!* Three more GI's jumped in our foxhole with us. I felt safer as it quickly became obvious that the whole company was finally awake.

Thup thup thup. Alright! The sweet sound of mortars. Light em' up, Indy.

Oh my God. Oh my God. With the sky all lit up, it looked like 100-200 gooks were coming our way. We were all emptying our magazines on the invading party, and they were dropping like flies. Six of them jumped over our foxhole, but they had no weapons.

Gator screams, "Zappers!!!"

"What the hell is a zapper?" I quickly and forcefully asked amongst the deafening sounds of rapid gunfire.

Then he quickly explained.

"Suicide squad. They are really called sappers, but this company calls them zappers because they zap you to death when they pull the charge. They infiltrate your area with explosives tied to their bodies and detonate themselves when they know they can kill as many GI's as possible."

After his rushed words I turned and shot one in the back, and then I saw the other zappers blow themselves up. *How many of us did they get? I'll figure that out later. No time for that now.*

It was at this time that our mortar platoon was laying some serious firepower on them. We all stayed in the foxholes until daylight, when the firing had long stopped and we were once again victorious.

The sun rose to a bloody field, and it was not a pretty sight. Looking out, we could see the ground littered with dead Charlies. Then we got the sad news. We had six dead soldiers, which were killed when the zappers detonated themselves as soon as they saw a few of us bunched together. That could have been me. Or Gator. Or Indy. Or *any* of us left alive.

We were all walking around in a daze. When we stopped, we rushed to see our dead. I only recognized one, from watching him reading his letters all the time with a smile firmly planted on his face. It was sadness personified. Although we fought like mad, it wasn't enough to save everyone. Afterwards, I found out that Sgt. Pete had killed two of the zappers with his bayonet, and Loner had also killed two by shooting them as they charged him.

When the medevac choppers arrived for our dead, you could see the somber expressions on everyone's faces. It was *so* sad. I didn't know any of these young men, but I felt so much pain for their families. Later, we did a body count of the enemy and we came up with seventy-six. Last night it looked like a *hundred* and seventy-six.

Overall, it was quite suspicious. I mean, here we were a mere hundred yards away from a village that said they never saw a Cong in over a year, but yet the night we come across the village we get attacked. A coincidence? *I think not.*

We were much too trusting. Now that the years have passed I know deep in my heart that the village we visited probably had informants telling the enemy where we were headed. But hindsight is 20-20. Sadly, at the time our focus was only one-sided and we just couldn't see the flip side of the coin. The only thing we thought about was that the artillery unit which we were headed to was probably overrun by the dead group of enemies that now spotted the landscape.

However, too much thinking was something that took time, and time we had little of that day. Before we could even make peace with what happened we were on our way towards the overrun artillery unit. Apparently it was a massacre, and we needed to claim the bodies of our fellow soldiers. You would think that the overwhelming essence of death would have overshadowed anything else, but it didn't. All I could think about was the dreaded five-mile jaunt in this extreme heat.

Just when I started to adequately prepare myself to toughen up, Top gathered us around and said we'd be flying there via Chinooks, our oversized choppers. The bodies had been out there way too long to wait on us any longer. Within fifteen minutes, three big Chinooks landed, and the back chute opened. The heat outside was so intense that we couldn't *wait* to get inside. Once we finally settled in the cargo area, which is basically just a massive, partially empty space, we were on our way. The trip was short, we landed quickly, and once the doors opened we were all overwhelmed with the unbearable stench of rotting flesh.

In plain view on a nearby hilltop we could see the bodies of our fellow GI's. They were all bloated from the extreme heat, causing many of us to heave our guts out, adding to the already wicked smells that coated the air. The smell was so bad that none of us could fully approach the hilltop with that overly noxious odor. We were quickly ordered to take our extra fatigues out of our backpacks and wrap them around our mouths and noses, which would help to alleviate the smell. To make things even worse, we were told by Sgt. Pete to stay in place for half an hour while he went over to talk to Top.

When he finally came back, which seemed like an eternity, he started talking to our Lieutenant, Jerry. The Lieutenant then asked who wanted to go with the Sarge and, as always, curiosity got the best of me and I volunteered. I followed him, and we both veered off to the right towards the jungle. *What the hell were we doing?*

Sarge stopped somewhat short of the hilltop, and quickly took out his machete. He then proceeded to cut three bamboo poles about ten foot each in length, and then reaches in his backpack to pull out a ball of twine. *Why would anyone carry twine out here?*

"Here, hold these two poles together," he orders.

After tying all of the ends together, voilà, we had a pole that was about thirty feet long. I took one end and he took the other and then we ventured to the top of the hill, with me dumbfounded the entire journey. *What is this guy doing?*

When we reached the top of the hill, it was one of the most horrific views I had ever seen. Twelve bloated, young American bodies were lying before me twisted in deathly agony, with all of them being unrecognizable as human beings. *How long were these people up here before we were able to reach them?*

Their presence, overall, had an equally bad response from my body. My eyes were watering like rain, and to this day I don't know whether it was from the odor of decaying flesh or knowing how they must have suffered before finally moving on. The only thing I was certain of was that this would be a closed casket funeral for every last one of these brave, young men.

As I crouched down in sorrow in a kind of mournful silence, I was at a complete loss as to what we were doing up here. It was obvious that these soldiers could no longer be helped. Before I could fully gauge the magnitude of the situation, Sarge abruptly interrupts my contemplative thoughts.

I was told to lay flat on my stomach in case the Cong booby trapped the bodies, which they were often known to do. From thirty feet away from the first body, I watched him poke the bamboo pole under the first GI and then turn him over, and we did that to the next eleven. *Damn, this guy was good.* If any of us greenhorns had touched these bodies, they could have been traps and we could've been going home prematurely along with these poor souls.

Once we were finished, we waved for the rest of the company to come topside, and many within my troop were still gagging, even though they had their mouths and noses covered. Six of our troops took the dead bodies to one of the awaiting Chinooks. After it left, another Chinook came and dropped chains and a harness so it could carry off the 105 artillery weapon. Overall, I was baffled why we had set down only twelve men in this terrain without infantry support.

To make matters even worse than they already seemed, we were going to be *stuck* in this horrible memory for a few more days since the Old Man said we were going to secure this area for a little while. On one hand, it was bad. But on the other, good, because the heat was unbearable and I was tired of traveling while soaking with sweat in places I didn't even know I had sweat glands.

However, sweat would be included anyway since we had a *lot* of work to do. So much for getting away from the heat. Although being on a hill was nice in a way, there were no foxholes dug, so that and our mortar pit was our number one priority. Everyone was chipping in, and after about four hours of rotating turns we finally had our perimeter completely dug and secure.

The next couple of days were spent writing letters and going around to the other platoons and getting to know one another. It's funny now that I think about it. Quite frankly, because of the number of diverse personalities between all of us and how extreme they were, you wouldn't think in a million years that we could all be friends. But in the heat of battle it was obvious we were more than that. We were brothers, which was something I wasn't accustomed to, but wholeheartedly welcomed because I was an only child. I never had the luxury of having a sibling, much less a whole platoon of them.

As time moved on with my newfound family and the third day arrived on this haunted hill of solace, the chopper that brought us our chow had a familiar face on it along with two new greenhorns. It was Elvis.

He walked by me and sarcastically asked, "You still alive?" Followed, of course, by a slight chuckling and a polite "Just kidding." I then watched him take the two new guys to Top and the Old Man. All of a sudden, for the first time since I've been here, I didn't feel like the new kid on the block anymore.

When Elvis returned to go back to the chopper, I asked, "You only brought us two to replace the six we lost?" He then informed me that we were going to be here several more days, and that he would probably show up with four more before our time here was up.

Time. You know, that word gets used a lot here. It's a funny thing, really. To most people time passes quickly, but during the war in Vietnam each hour lasted a day, especially on this dreary hill. But we all made the best of it shooting the breeze with one another. It's hard to believe that we were having a little fun on a place that once reeked of violence and death. We sat for days on soil that contained the blood of people's sons and fathers. But life has to move on. It must.

On the fourth day, moving on didn't seem like it was enough, and monotony definitely set in. Indy could sense that, so he casually stated that they had to unload all the mortar rounds because we were getting a new supply of them. He wanted to know if I wanted to shoot off a few. Of *course* I wanted to! Let me think. A late teen soldier and high powered explosives. What did he *think* the answer was going to be?

Once he started in, I finally got to see Indy in action, and was quickly made aware of what he could actually do. Although the 4th platoon worked with precision as a group, it was Indy with his plotting board that made it all happen. He showed me how he calculated the degree with the distance, which was basically like he was talking algebra and geometry at the same time so he may as well have been speaking Greek. After nodding my head incessantly due to false understanding, and watching about six rounds drop down the chute, it was finally *my* turn.

Thup thup thup. This was fun. We could see and hear the rounds explode in the open space beyond us. But then the unexpected happened. I dropped one down the chute, and it went straight up about fifty feet and just kind of hung there.

Without knowing what I was about to do to myself I yelled, "Short Round!"

Everyone scattered and, fortunately, it was a dud and didn't go off. From that day on out my nickname was Short Round. I knew I'd get one eventually, but did it *have* to be something that also had the word short in it? For the next two days, it seemed like everyone wanted to call me that name. Surprisingly, I think it helped me to bond with a lot of the GI's. It's as if it made them feel more comfortable because they finally had something they could call me other than *hey you*.

As the hours and even days passed we all joked and laughed, which was all we could do until the waiting game changed directions. I think it started to become a time of enjoyment because we all started to feel somewhat safe. Our choppers even came in with supplies three times a day since we were stationary, so that helped as well. I felt an extreme amount of companionship with my fellow troops during this moment of calm, and it was at this particular time that I felt completely disconnected from the outside world.

Then, without warning, something happened that allowed me to reconnect. It was mail call, and my name was finally announced. I received four letters from mom and dad, and three letters from my wife, and I was quickly on top of the world. They missed me so much, and everything they said reminded me of how much I missed them as well. Surprisingly enough, my step-dad even wrote, and it sounded like he was extremely proud of me.

My wife kept talking about the anticipation of our son being born. Gosh, now I could finally see why everyone in the company cherished mail call so much. In addition to letters, many also received care packages of cookies, candy, and beef jerky, amongst other things. I was so incredibly happy to be re-connected, and it was this first string of letters that made me realize why I had to protect myself at all costs. For the moment, that is. As with everything pertaining to youthful recklessness, my thoughts of self-protection would be short lived.

But for now? I didn't have to worry about it. *Or did I?* After five days of peace came and went, the company was getting restless because they were getting too complacent. They knew being comfortable in such an unpredictable land was a really bad thing. In addition, they were also a little hungry for action. When you move around as much as we did, sitting still for too long can make you a bit eager to get up and go.

However, before we did we all had time to reflect and really get to know the people we were with. For me, it was at this time that I also had a better gauge of how the rest of my troops really looked, especially now that we were out in the open in the dreadful blaze of the bright sun.

Overall, these guys all looked ten years older than me, but the only ones who actually *were* that old were the Sergeants and the Old Man. But I was used to it, always being shorter, skinnier, and younger looking than everyone as I was growing up. In addition, the harshness of the summer sun, the dirt, and the often unshaven look of most of these guys easily hid any signs of youthfulness that existed underneath.

The only time I had a chance not to feel like the baby of the troop was when two new guys came in that looked like they were sixteen, even though I knew they couldn't be. Compared to everyone else they had the look of a kindergarten child starting his first day of school. It was at that particular time that I was starting to finally feel like an old timer. I guess in a way I was, especially considering I was starting to sense when the upper brass wanted to move on and get down to business.

"Get ready to take off tomorrow," Sgt. Pete barked to our ever-eager platoon.

It was time to move, but that was okay because it was a good week. No casualties, no stress, and the unexpected words from home were great. But man was I bored out of my skull. It was *definitely* time to go.

The next morning three choppers were coming our way, but why three? The first dropped our chow to us. I saw the second one drop off three more greenhorns, and the third had Elvis and another greenhorn. Our three new recruits from the second chopper ran up to us like scared little children. I remember feeling like that.

From the third chopper a heavy set greenhorn stepped out, and then everyone was startled to hear the sound of an AK-47. It sounded like fireworks. He just got hit in the leg by a sniper, and I saw Elvis dragging him back in the chopper. The Viet Cong, safely hidden in the trees off in the distance, had done his job. Quickly, we all took our positions on the hill, and then watched the door gunner do his thing when the chopper took off. Man, was he *ever* blasting that tree line. I hope he got him.

An hour later, we were almost ready to take off when another helicopter arrives. I watched the door gunner get out with a piece of paper and walk directly up to the Old Man. *What's going on?* Then he walks over to Loner, who had long been staying in the background and out of trouble since I took over his job, and shook his hand. *Everyone* was shaking his hand and patting him on the back. *Oh no. He's going home.* I was so sad, both for myself as well as the rest of my company, but overjoyed for ***him***.

As soon as I walked up to him the first words out of his mouth were, "Thank you, Short Round." Then we hugged and he told me not to do anything foolish.

"The company is in good hands with you aboard," he firmly stated.

Overall, you could see the jubilation on his face due to the fact that he was going home. What a guy. He was one of my mentors along with Gator and Indy, and as he got on the chopper I knew that was probably the last I would ever see of him. I wish him well.

After the chopper took off into the distant sky, Top walked to the top of the hill. Sounding almost like

General McArthur from days gone by, he confidently spoke his next order.

"Saddle up!" Then, surprisingly, he also signaled for me before speaking his next words.

"Head us in the direction of where that sniper went, but be careful. ***He could still be out there***."

Once I heard my assignment, I looked down and saw that Lifer was at my heels. The Old Man told me to take her with me and that she wouldn't bark. It was kind of risky, but I went along with it. I just couldn't believe that he was letting her out of his sight.

As I moved through the jungle, she and I weren't ten minutes in the bush when I noticed that her tongue was really hanging out due to all of this heat. So I stopped and got my canteen out and kept pouring water into my hand until her thirst was quenched. After another ten minutes passed out of the blue she stopped dead in her tracks. Her fur went straight up and she started to growl this vicious sounding growl.

Proceeding with the utmost of caution, I eventually noticed a Cong lying on his back. He was covered with blood and his AK-47 was right beside him. Lifer circled him like a lion eyeing its prey, and continued to growl. Still alive, he quickly spots me. In slow motion he reaches for his weapon. I unload three or four rounds on him, and he was instantly dead.

It was obvious that I was no longer the boy who was trained to be a man by his stepfather. Instead, I was a man who was fighting for survival because of it. On one hand, I was stunned at what I had just done so easily. But I felt no remorse, because if I wouldn't have done it he would've easily done it to me.

I picked up Lifer and gave her a hug, because I truly believe to this day that she had saved my life by alerting me that he was there. After being coated by dog saliva for three minutes, the company was there in a flash. They had feared the worst after hearing those shots. When they arrived Top had a big old smile on his face and the rest were chanting, "Short Round." Sgt. Pete quickly told them to shut up.

The Old Man asked what happened, and I told him that Lifer may have just saved my life. He picked her up and said, "Well, that's what I recruited her for." Between the door gunner of the chopper doing his job and Lifer, I was still in an upright position. I was very thankful to still be alive.

Due to my accomplishment, I didn't pull point the rest of the day. We only walked about a mile more, and then we set up camp in a pretty remote area. From the looks of things, American soldiers were there a few days or maybe even a week before us.

During this time it looked as though we were trying to figure out what our next move was. The CO was always talking on the telephone that the RTO had on his person. I can't see how they carry that unit around all day. I've picked up those gadgets and they're pretty darned heavy, especially considering you have to carry the rest of your equipment as well.

Once we finally got settled in our new position and supplies started coming in on a regular basis, I started eagerly awaiting mail call again. It was at this point that my letters started coming in like clockwork. *Man, I really miss home.*

As I'm writing a letter, a new greenhorn comes over and sits beside me. It kind of reminds me of when I first sat down next to Loner.

"Can I help you?" I asked.

Speaking with a strong Northeastern accent, but in a rather articulate way, he said he would like to be a point man and wanted to learn from me. He was from Boston, and his thick accent caused me to chuckle a bit because the more he talked the more his words became hysterical. You have to remember, I'm from the Midwest. We sound a little different there.

Even though I tried to warn him of all the dangers that came with being a point man, he was extremely adamant on being one. Which was fine with me. Although I had been doing this just a short time, I was ready to relinquish being up front. So I took him to Sgt. Pete, and after getting it cleared with the greenhorn's platoon leader as well as Top and the Old Man, his journey with me would begin the very next day.

Not without instruction, of course. The rest of the daylight hours were spent telling him what to expect, which would continue for the next four days before and after our work on point. Although he seemed to listen to everything that I told him, for four days it was the same old thing so it's not like we had a lot of obstacles to face. When we ventured out we had *no* confrontations with the enemy and didn't really come across *anything*, so his training was a *lot* easier than mine was.

Overall, he seemed a little cocky, almost to the point of arrogance, but I thought that maybe it could turn into something good. *I was wrong.*

It all started when he wanted to go out on his own. Truthfully, I thought he could handle it. I told our leaders that he would be okay, so off he went. After about ten minutes passed we decided to follow his path of broken branches and twigs. All seemed fine, but about thirty minutes later we heard a blood-curdling scream, and it sounded like he was being tortured.

When we arrived, which was in a matter of seconds, we saw that he had fallen in a punji pit. It was about four foot deep, and in the pit were bamboo sticks that were sharpened on the end, which made them resemble wooden razor blades. He had fallen in since it was camouflaged with grass and banana leaves. The razor like points were covered in buffalo dung to infect the wound, and the one he had fallen on went into the arch of his foot and out the calf of his leg.

Sgt. Pete took immediate action, reached down and cut the base of the chutes, and then six guys helped him out of the pit. He was screaming, and one of our four medics came over and shot him up with morphine. After that he was in na na land, and ten minutes later a medevac chopper came and picked him up. As we stood around watching the helicopter take off in the distance, I pointed out that he took a *very* used trail to get back instead of following procedure by using the trail he just made. *Damn.* I told him over and over to never use a well-taken trail.

With my apprentice screwing up big time, the next day I was back at it again. Leading the pack and pulling point, and being more careful now than ever after witnessing that punji pit. On and on, day after day, with each and every day getting hotter and hotter.

One day, in the mid morning hours, we were all sweltering in this hellacious land to the point where we all looked like sweat-covered Zombies. It must have been 120 degrees, and our whole company was out of water. The choppers weren't going to be with us for at least six more hours. *How in the hell were we to survive this heat without water*?

Walking back to the company from my position, I see Sgt. Pete walking towards me, but looking straight up. His eyes were focused on the branches of the looming trees that were above us. All of a sudden, a big old smile emerges as he pulls down a vine and tells me to come over.

"Watch this, Short Round," he confidently says. With his machete, he slices open a vine and cool, clean water starts gushing right out of it.

He motions for me to fill up my canteen, and then he did the same. The whole company started slicing vines, but no luck. Sgt. Pete was the only one who knew which ones to cut into. Once he did more, by the time it was all over with he had managed to fill up every last canteen for the whole company.

This guy is amazing. I asked him what his secret was, but he wouldn't tell me. In my opinion, I think he really liked the fact that he knew how to do something the others didn't.

When our thirst was finally quenched, time moved on. Slowly. No action, no excitement, and nothing new. Until another week or so went by. It was around this time that I started to train a new man for point. He was very soft spoken, but had the demeanor of a hit man. They called him Burns, and he never would tell me what the nickname stood for. Unlike the last guy, he became very good at point, and was always asking me questions, which made me feel good because I always had the answers thanks to Loner.

With a new man at point finally trained, all seemed well for me. In a way, I suppose. A lot less stressful, of course, but also a *lot* more boring. Many days passed and we saw little or no action. Actually, we had many days in a row when we couldn't even find a village.

Then one day Burns returned to our company saying he had spotted a village and that it looked friendly. As we approached it, we noticed a lot of elderly villagers, and the smell of marijuana was utterly overwhelming. You can never mistake that smell since it kind of smells like a skunk, but this stuff was *extremely* noxious, like an army of skunks. *Wow, a person could really get high off of this stuff.* Indy told me that they harvest it themselves, and it is *much* more potent than what you can get stateside.

It showed. Kit tried talking to several of the villagers, but said that they were all stoned. I can sure see why, because I'm just standing here smelling the stuff from a distance and I'm feeling dizzy.

After a little time passes and I begin to slowly sway back and forth, I notice that two old ladies are talking a million miles an hour with Kit. *And here I thought people who spoke Spanish talked fast.*

When he finally returns to the Old Man, he states that they are concerned about their two very young daughters. They usually play down in a tunnel for about an hour, but they have been down there almost three. The Old Man tells Kit that it is not our concern, but since he has three daughters of his own he would love to somehow help.

He gathered everyone around and tells all of us the circumstances, and asked if anyone would like to volunteer. All eyes shifted to me, and I know why. *Let's send the little crazy guy* is probably what they were all thinking. I can't believe that I said I'll go. *What the hell was **I** thinking?*

The Old Man then proceeds to tell me that going down in the underground tunnels that were often built is the number one suicide mission that I had always wondered about.

"It's all volunteer," he somberly spoke. That's when Gator and Indy quickly spoke up.

"He aint going" was said in unison.

After watching the bickering going back and forth between my two mentors and the Old Man, I finally spoke up and said, "I want to go."

Actually, I was just curious what it was like to go underground. In addition, I suppose part of me also wanted to help because I saw the two old ladies crying. I tell you, between my curiosity, my eagerness to please, and wanting to show people what I could do, I'm surprised I didn't get killed the first day I was here. Well, here I was, again, purposefully stepping on that plank before even *looking* out to sea.

When my new underground job started, I had no idea that this would be the start of something. On this day the goal was innocent, but on future days…not so much.

Today, however, was an easy one. We walked over to an isolated area, and one of the women pointed downwards. I couldn't see any kind of entryway. Then she got down on her knees and pointed to what we call a spider hole or, basically, a hidden foxhole. It was covered by a self-made bamboo mat that was partially hidden by the dirt.

After I started to crawl in, I noticed that my backpack and M16 were too awkward to handle, so Top took those from me and handed me his 45 pistol. It wasn't until he asked for my dog tags (Metal identification tags that we hung around our necks) that I realized the seriousness of the situation I was getting myself into. Firmly, and in a stone cold voice, he spoke.

"If you don't come back, we aren't coming down there to get you."

Armed with a flashlight in one hand and the 45 in the other, I slowly crawled on my belly like a snake. The light that shined into the distance showed no end in sight. *How in the hell has a tunnel been dug this far?* After three minutes or so, I noticed how cool and comfortable it was. I also noticed that I could now crawl on my hands and knees. Another five minutes went by and I could hear giggles. Instantly I turned off my flashlight, just in case. As I got closer to the sound, I could see two small figures with a lantern playing happily in the dirt.

Once I turned my own light back on they started screaming and crying and were, obviously, scared to death. Trying to smile, I waved to them, speaking in a soft voice, hoping it would make them feel more comfortable. Finally, they came to me, and I gave them both a hug and pointed to the way out. I allowed them to go first with their lantern, and when we were on the outside mama-san let them have it. I guess time just got away from them, but I knew why they went down there because it was a heck of a lot cooler embedded deep in the Earth when compared to the sweltering heat of the outside.

Top gave me back my M16, backpack, and dog tags, and once I gave him his 45 back he said, "Your 45 and holster will be on the next supply chopper." Sure enough, late that afternoon, the supply chopper had my 45 on its list.

For the rest of our stay in the village, we decided to secure it. I spent the next couple of hours in our hooch, cleaning my rifle, and practicing over and over disassembling my 45. It didn't need cleaned since it looked brand new, and I suppose I didn't need to practice disassembling it so much, but I was trained to always be prepared for a weapons jam. When I finished practicing, Indy said he never saw anyone take apart and reassemble a 45 that fast, which made me feel really good since I had so much respect for my two hooching buddies.

Since I had a moment to talk with Indy, I asked him something I had been meaning to for quite some time. Every day I watched soldiers get on the choppers, without being wounded, and taking off only to return in a week.

"What's with *that*?" I asked Indy.

"After you are in country for six months, you can apply for R and R," he responded. He also told me that most of the married guys go to Hawaii to meet their wives, and the others go to Thailand, Australia, and Bangkok. Wow, now I *really* have something to look forward to.

Later on, as the conversations dwindled due to exhaustion, and the evening came to a close, we were told that we would be seeing some pretty heavy action tomorrow. The choppers would be dropping us off in a hot zone loaded with VC. We also learned that the area in question, which is another village, has been hit hard with our jets dropping Napalm all over it. Napalm is a substance that burns, and also takes your breath away.

Overall, I didn't sleep well that night, because I have never been dropped off by a helicopter while action was actually going on. It was on my mind all evening, and it was all I could think about, even when I had guard duty with Gator. Once the next morning arrived, our choppers landed with chow and water. Shortly afterwards we were told the oh-so-fun details on what we should *probably* expect.

Lieutenant Jerry and Sgt. Pete from our platoon gathered all of us around, and so did all of the other leaders of their respective platoons. Then they showed us maps of the terrain. Although it looks like it had a *little* bit of jungle, it was mostly open area.

We will be going in right after the first platoon, and our job is to charge the village, even though most of the village has been destroyed by the bombs and the napalm. However, even then, supposedly there's still a lot of Cong around. *Supposedly*.

We were all silently jacked and scared at the same time. Most of us just wanted to get this over with. But before it could happen, we had to wait for our transportation. When it finally came, it looked like a convoy of choppers was headed towards us. They were everywhere.

The first platoon got on their choppers and took off. We were next. I jumped on our chopper with Gator, Indy, and three others. My adrenaline was pumping, and I was extremely hyped because I just didn't know what to expect. It seemed like we were in the air for half an hour or so. Unexpectedly, the pilot says to get ready because we were going in.

All of a sudden the door gunner is lighting it up with his machine gun, and at the same time I can hear bullets hitting the steel frame of our chopper. The pilot says he can't land and we'll have to jump. We're hovering twenty feet above the ground, so I couldn't believe what we were being told to do.

The first three jumped, and I could see two of them holding their ankles afterwards. Gator said it's time to go. The three of us stood on the skids, and Indy and Gator took my wrists and lowered me as far as they could before they released me. I guess they figured since I was the smallest of the bunch I'd have a much farther drop. When I looked up, as my two friends were dropping to the ground I noticed that the door gunner was slouched over. Apparently he had just been hit. The chopper took off, and the rest of our company in the remaining choppers had to do what we just did with an array of bullets being aimed their direction. *Holy shit, I thought they had destroyed this village. I guess not.*

Just then, the gunfire ceased, so I'm guessing one of our door gunners managed to pick off whoever was firing at us. Soon afterwards, as soon as his feet touched the ground Top started barking his orders. Everyone was paying close attention because no one really knew what was going on.

Once things settled down, we found out that except for our door gunner and perhaps a few others that we're unaware of on the choppers, we didn't have any casualties. All we suffered were just a few sprained ankles.

That's when we started to move. Carefully, we approached the village as if we were in the dense jungle. This wasn't a regular village, and seemed rather different in a way because it contained an overabundance of huts, one after the next. It was almost as if it was some sort of Cong base camp. It was *much* more than what we were accustomed to seeing.

What was even stranger was all of the dead bodies, looking as if they were still alive. They were sitting down, often in natural poses, and burnt to a crisp. Some were covered in white ash, and others just looked like they were asleep. That napalm was *fierce*. It was, overall, an extremely eerie sight, and reminded me of images I had seen in National Geographic. The issue in question showed the once-ash covered Roman bodies that were buried in Pompeii after the eruption of Mt. Vesuvius. Just like those early ancestors, these people were stuck frozen in time and they had *no* idea what hit them.

I shook my head fiercely, trying to snap out of it. My mission was clear, and I had to be focused by concentrating on the living, not the dead. We were to check every hut, and shoot to kill anything that moved. It seems like we checked everywhere, and it seemed clear, but if so, where were those that shot at us when we were landing?

Hours went by, with us exploring every last inch of that village. Nothing.

Just as we were about to give up hope, two soldiers from the first platoon drag out a very old man who acted like he was on another planet. He was stoned out of his mind. Kit went up to him and started slapping him and yelling questions. Still, no response. Our ***own*** Old Man gets on the horn and calls something in. The next thing I know, the next chopper arrives and it contains a dog handler with the biggest German Shepard I have ever seen. It's funny, but I had no idea we even *had* dog units over here.

The handler tells us not to pet the dog or we might lose our hand. We all wanted to because he was absolutely beautiful. Lifer was wagging her tail, and starts to belly up to the big dog. The handler quickly tells the company Commander that we better keep her away, because his dog might easily destroy her.

After a short time passes, the old villager is brought to the handler. He's got this creature on a very thick leash, and starts to slowly walk near him. Kit continues to ask him question, but not once did he get a response. The handler tells Kit to tell him he's going to unleash his dog unless he gets the information they need.

Surprisingly enough, the guy never says one damn word. So the handler gives a command, and that dog jumped at that old geezer with his mouth open and the sharpest, razor like teeth in the world. It was scary. The ferocity of this beast got within two inches of the guy's face, and then the handler pulled back on the leash.

Obviously this Viet Cong was stoned beyond belief, because he never even blinked. Over and over again this was repeated. Kit kept slapping, and the dog kept lunging. Finally, Top told us to detain him and we'll talk to him tomorrow once the dope has finally worn off.

Until that time comes, we decided to make camp on the very outskirts of the village, because even though we searched the best we could, who knows how many are still in there hiding, perhaps even underground. The night passed, slowly, and we were all on edge. It wasn't just knowing they were still out there. For some, it was also because we were right next to a town filled to the brim with mummified, charred remains that made us feel like we were sleeping next to a living nightmare. I wonder if that's how some people in Nagasaki and Hiroshima looked during World War II after the blasts. It was frightening, to say the least.

We all tried not to think about it, but as the next morning finally arrived, it was quite obvious that hardly any of us got a millisecond of sleep. Lucky for us, we were quickly jolted out of our euphoric drowsiness and into the present when our choppers arrived with a much-needed hot breakfast. They wouldn't land last night because way too much was going on.

It was at this time that the pilot informed us that our door gunner who got shot had died, and he only had two weeks to go before he went home, too. Now he gets to go home early, but in a body bag. Because of this, the whole company is pissed beyond belief. Where in the hell is that old Viet Cong? We *all* wanted some answers.

After breakfast was over with, we started back towards the huts, thinking it was time to question the old villager again. All of a sudden shooting breaks out and a soldier yells out in pain.

Sgt. Pete starts screaming for the medics. I rush to see, and oh my God. My designated platoon leader has just been shot in the chest. I'm watching Sgt. Pete with his fingers in Jerry's chest as he tells him to hang on.

"Just hang on. You're not going to die. I've stopped the bleeding," he said.

Just then, our machine gunner spots three Cong and takes all of them out by himself. *Damn, please hang on Jerry.* This was one sweetheart of a guy. Usually Lieutenants are certified A-holes, but not Jerry. He was everyone's friend, and most definitely wasn't your typical 2nd Lieutenant.

We all stood there, watching Sgt. Pete in action, and you could just see how intent he was on saving this man's life. As he screamed for the medics, he told Top to get a medevac helicopter ASAP. In a mere five minutes the medevac arrives. The amount of support we get when we really need it is unbelievable.

After the chopper lands, eight guys carry Jerry to it, with the Sarge running along beside him with his fingers still in Jerry's chest. He boards the chopper with him, and I and the rest of the company are in total awe of this man. He was doing whatever it took to save his friend.

The chopper took off, and we were all *extremely* angry over this latest happening. With a dead door gunner, and now our platoon leader on death's door, we wanted answers. Again, we brought out the old villager, and now that he was no longer stoned the dog handler was going to try again.

Kit starts slapping him around, and he *does* start cowering a little bit, giving us an indication that he's much more aware of what's going on compared to yesterday. Then the dog handler gives the command, and I swear that dog came half an inch from ripping his face off.

Man, he started chirping like a magpie. Kit wanted to know how many were left in the village and where they were. In his Vietnamese language he kept saying, "Underground."

Indy looked at me and said, "Don't even think about it."

Stupidity or Bravery: What Did I Have to Prove?

All day long the old villager was showing Kit, Top, and our Old Man where all the tunnels were. Gator kept telling me that my wife was waiting back home, obviously in an attempt to get me to change my mind if I was asked to go underground since it was something I could easily refuse. I couldn't, because youthful curiosity, again, got the best of me. Add that to wanting to prove that I could do it, and you have a game of Russian roulette in the making. But before I would potentially take my underground journey, I had to wait one more night, which was a chore for everyone because we all knew the enemy was close by.

After a dreadfully slow and nerve-racking evening, the choppers arrived in the morning. In addition to getting two new recruits, Sgt. Pete had returned and he was smiling from ear to ear.

"Jerry is going to be alright," he proudly stated. He had every reason to be proud. We all knew that it was the Sarge who had saved his life. As everyone was giving him their congratulations, I was called out.

"Short round, the Commander wants to talk to you."

As I walked towards my destination, I noticed that Indy, Gator, and Sgt. Pete were all walking right behind me. I knew what was coming.

The Old Man tells me to sit, and then informs me that the old VC (Which we found out he actually was) told us that there are many tunnels that run under this village. Some are big, and some are small, but many of them have VC still in them. It was quite a scary thought, knowing we had been sleeping right above the enemy for days.

Sure, it was my choice whether or not I wanted to go after them. It was a suicide mission with only a 50-50 chance of survival, but the choice was all mine and mine alone. He said that if I said no he would understand completely and then we'd be on our merry little way. However, if I said yes I'd be on my own, because no one else was willing to go down there.

Gator and Indy responded with a quick and completely in sync, "Hell no" as they were looking at me, hoping that I would agree. Sgt. Pete just shrugged his shoulders and looked at me. I asked Pete if he'd come with me and, again, I heard the words, "Hell no."

I look at the Old Man, who is looking at the ground, and I confidently spoke.

"Yeah. Hell, yeah. I'll do it."

Again, as he's done many times before, Indy slapped me upside my helmet. I don't blame him, really. There's a fine line between bravery and stupidity, and I kept crossing it.

Top and the Old Man showed me many of the tunnels and asked me to pick one. I just randomly pointed to the closest one to us. Gator held my M16, ammo clip to my rifle, and my backpack and dog tags, and then I armed myself with a 45 in one hand and a flashlight in the other. As I turned around, I noticed that half the company was staring at me in a very solemn way. Almost as if they thought this was the last time they would ever see me. All the while they were telling me to be careful and wishing me good luck.

So down I went. I entered on my belly, and after only ten feet in I was completely surprised at the fact that I was almost able to stand up. *Just how in the world do they get all of this dirt out of here?* It had to take them years.

At first, I started to become a little disappointed, because the light of my flashlight shining ahead showed nothing but a dead end. But as I started to turn around and go back I hear someone, and it sounds like they're singing. I couldn't figure it out, because it didn't seem like there was a way to reach the voice. However, as I took off towards it, I noticed that there was an almost hidden, sharp bend to the left that could easily be overlooked. My flashlight quickly turned off by the quick reaction of my hand, and as I waited patiently I saw a shadow coming off a light from a lantern.

He has his back towards me, and I walked as quietly as a mouse in order to get closer and closer. I was literally one foot from him when he turned around, spots me, and tries to grab a hold of my wrist. The trigger of my gun was something I didn't even hesitate to pull. I shot him, twice, and he instantly falls like a rock. Unfortunately, I can't hear a damn thing after that. It was so loud and at such close range in a closed off area that it was like someone had poured water into my ears and then plugged them up to give it no chance to escape.

Afterwards, I sat down beside his lifeless body, and thought of what I had just done. In the pre-soldier days, this probably would have affected me. But I was now a soldier, and I felt no remorse. I felt no sorrow. This was war, pure and simple, and a death on their side meant fewer deaths on ours. Since my fellow soldiers had become family, this was important to me. Families are meant to be protected at all costs.

All I could think about was that this might have been the guy who shot Jerry. I looked at his features, and I no longer saw a fellow human being. All I could see was a very evil looking young man.

When my senses were partially regained, I knew that my job in this hole was done. I took his AK-47 with me so I could show the guys the reason they probably heard a gunshot. When I arrived back in the open air, guys were talking to me left and right, but I had a hard time hearing them. Everything just echoed. Gator came over and picked me up in a great big bear hug. Indy, again, slapped my helmet.

Once I was finally able to hear again, I overheard Sgt. Pete saying, "Short Round, you are *one* crazy little man."

Because of all that adrenaline and praise I was pumped. As scary as it is to say, I actually wanted *more*. Top said I could go down one more today if I wanted to, but it was time to eat some C-rations first. After I inhaled my lunch, I was itching to do it again.

It's funny now that I think about it. To some, this would seem to be the epitome of bravery and proving ones worth, which is probably what I was thinking at the time. To others, it would seem like more chances to die or end up deaf. To me, I'm guessing it was more along the lines of proving my worth. *Again, thanks a lot, Dad!* Ah. The follies of youth. Getting young people killed since the dawn of time. Whatever the case may be, I was fully ready and willing to venture into the next tunnel. I was set on it, and no one was going to talk me out of it. So here I go again.

Before I entered the new hole to this underground lair, I noticed that it seemed to be quite a bit bigger at the opening. As I entered, I approached in the exact same manner as the last one, but I was only in twenty feet before I was actually able to stand straight up.

To keep myself safe, I kept shining my flashlight for about three seconds and turning it off for about thirty. This went on for what seemed like an eternity. All of a sudden, I see a glimpse of light about twenty-five to thirty yards away. At this time my flashlight is totally off, and I inch myself towards the light. Then I hear voices. *Oh my God, here we go again.*

Once I get to where I thought the voices were coming from, I see a monster sized pit that was dug down below. It was a huge room that had a ladder made of bamboo leading down towards it. I looked over the edge and there were two gooks, smoking their weed of course. The room had all kinds of things in it. In one corner I saw a stack of AK-47s, and in the other areas I spied bandages and maps but, most of all, *many* containers of rice. This was a combination of a hospital, food supply unit, and a strong supply of Viet Cong intelligence.

Okay, how long should I wait here? These guys didn't look like they were going anywhere any time soon, and I sure as hell wasn't going to climb down that ladder. I'd be dead in a heartbeat. So I waited. I knew my company would think something was wrong if I didn't turn up in a little while, but something was telling me that this room was important. Fifteen minutes went by, and just as I was about to give up and turn back, one of the VC stood up and headed towards the ladder. Then the other one followed right behind him.

I laid silently towards the edge, because I knew my best hope was to shoot as soon as one got to the top. In my estimation, I figured both of them would be too occupied climbing the ladder to be able to return fire quickly enough.

Here they come. Once the first one reached up and put his hands on the ledge, I lunged forward and shot him between the eyes. As he was falling backwards, I made a quick lunge to shoot the other, and shot him once in the head, but I only grazed him, so I shot him two more times.

Shaking like a leaf in the wind, I looked down into the pit at their lifeless bodies. As I climbed down the ladder, I noticed that my senses once again had escaped me. I couldn't hear crap. Plus, I hurt my hand on my helmet with the recoil from my gun, because I was unable to keep my elbow locked when I shot the second time around.

Trying to overcome my deafness and pain, I looked around the room in awe, and was completely amazed at what I saw. *Oh my word, I have never seen so many weapons.* In addition, I saw so many barrels of rice you could've literally fed an entire army. Last, but certainly not least, documents were everywhere.

For some strange reason I decided to put my hands through some of the barrels of rice, and I felt even *more* paper. As I quickly found out, it was more documents and maps, and I bet myself that these were the *really* important ones. Otherwise they wouldn't have been trying to hide them. So I stuffed my fatigue pockets with all the paperwork that I could handle, completely loaded down with bits of paper that were written in a language that I couldn't even begin to comprehend.

Once I made my way to the surface, everyone was just sitting there, with a look on their faces like they had just seen a ghost. *I'll be damned.* The company Commander even had tears in his eyes.

"Sir, you're a big cry baby," I jokingly announced. Everyone laughed. Top said that they had heard a total of four shots since I was down there and thought that it was all over for me.

As I described what I saw, I proceeded to bring all of the papers out of my pockets. The Old Man said we hit the jackpot. He brought Kit over to translate, and we found out that they were destination points and times. Basically, I had recovered pre-determined attacks that were going to occur.

The Old Man smiled and said, "Short Round, I am now making you an E4. Plus whatever other award I see fitting. Paperwork will be sent on the next chopper out."

Hey, a pay raise for my wife. I was elated. It wasn't over yet, though, because the Old Man wanted me to go back down there and blow all of that rice up.

"But sir, I've had very minimal experience in that field," I quickly reminded him.

"That's okay, Bill will show you," he replied. With an obviously puzzled look on my face I asked who Bill was.

Indy speaks up with a pretty clear-cut summary. "He's in the 4th platoon and a great guy. Super with explosives."

Top then gets on the horn and orders four bricks of C4 to be on the next chopper. Indy then introduces me to Bill. He has a great personality, and he and I hit it off right off the bat. He wasn't much taller than I am, which is a rare thing at barely five foot two, but he was incredibly stocky.

His origin state was Minnesota, and his father was in construction demolition. That's how he knew what he knew. Overall, it seemed as though his dad taught him absolutely everything that would allow him to survive. That sounds vaguely familiar.

Later that day, as the choppers arrived, sure enough there were four bricks of C4, wiring, blasting caps, and a detonator on them. As soon as he saw them, Bill took control and hooked everything together. I had to carry them in my backpack, which I didn't have the last two times because all I had was my 45 and a flashlight. Lucky for us, this tunnel was a lot taller than most of them, or I wouldn't have been able to get through.

Bill kept the detonator, because it's always a good idea to keep that separate from the other materials as you're transporting them. Once I proceeded to my destination, I was told to empty the containers and place the bricks under the piles of rice. It was kind of eerie stepping over the two dead bodies, but I tried not to let it bother me. After spending about ten minutes of emptying all the rice, I placed the C4 where Bill told me to. As I was doing so, I found a few more documents, so I put them in my pocket and then I was finally on my way.

Once we were both outside, Bill squeezed the detonator. Man, what a noise *that* was. I wanted to go back and look at the damage, but the Old Man said no. In addition, as crazy as it sounds and, believe me, now that I look back it does seem crazy, I also wanted to go back down more tunnels.

I wouldn't get the chance, because we were told we had to move out and we were going to break from camp in about an hour and a half. This was something I couldn't figure out. Why would we leave this destination when there were probably more Charlies down in the tunnels? It just didn't make any sense to me.

However, it soon did. As soon as we were three hundred yards from our last destination, I turned around and saw the air force jets bombing the hell out of the village we had just come from and, literally, turning it into a parking lot. I highly doubt anything even *below* ground could have survived *that*.

After traveling a short while, we broke for camp by securing an area that was previously occupied by GI's. I was bored here, so I began to look for Bill to have someone somewhat new to talk with. He was a great guy, really, but that's no surprise since most people there actually were. They were the most friendly, welcoming, and complimentary people I think I've ever met. As an example, as I made my way across camp I constantly heard, "Hey, Short Round, great job!" which, of course, made me feel like awesome sauce personified.

Finally, after my head was about to explode from becoming too big due to all of the overwhelming praise, I found Bill, and the new conversations began. Man, we talked about everything. He was from Paul Bunyan land, as he affectionately called it.

"Ten thousand lakes, and that's a low estimate," he says.

He wasn't married, lived at home, and works for his dad's business.

"You'll have to come visit me up in Minnesota someday," he genuinely remarked.

"I would love that," I happily replied. *Heck, anything to get myself out a giant corn field for a while in central Illinois would definitely be a good thing.*

Just as the conversation started to wind down, another guy I hadn't met made his appearance, and Bill introduced him to me as Oreo. Which was funny, really, because he didn't look like he was a mixed race. As I looked up I saw an extremely baby faced kid, with the biggest smile you have ever seen. I do remember seeing him once or twice, and even saw him get off the chopper a while back when he was first coming into our company.

While he started talking about anything and everything, all I could think about was why they called him Oreo. Maybe he ate cookies all the time that his parents sent him in goodie bags. The suspense was killing me.

"Why Oreo?" I asked.

"I'm from Oregon," he replied. *Now that's a strange way to get a nickname.*

After a quick laugh, we talked until the choppers came in, and my new friends kept asking me questions about going down in the tunnels. Truthfully, I felt uneasy talking about it, so I changed the subject to my wife, and things got a little bit more relaxed. Overall, it was great to find two more good friends. They were nothing like Gator and Indy, but they were still both *really* great guys.

As I got to know these two great people, time marched on like molasses like it often did in the bush, but at least it was pleasant this time. After all, now it was about getting to know new people and no action that could risk our lives. It's funny how often I wished for *no* action to be safe, but yet when I had the opportunity for it I never hesitated to turn it down. Which doesn't surprise me since my life has always been a constant state of confusion. My time in Vietnam was no different. But for now? Confusion was not a factor. For at least a little while I and the rest of my company had peace.

On the other hand, don't assume that life was *all* sunshine and puppy dogs. We did have our fair share of depressing circumstances, mainly due to the weather. Over a period of the next few days, we had a *ton* of rain. I thought it was monsoons that hit us, but Sgt. Pete said this was just a drizzle, all the while laughing uncontrollably. That means he must've witnessed the building of an Ark to have seen worse.

However, one morning, after being bombarded by a non-stop array of wetness, the rains *finally* slowed down. As the heavens opened up and we could see the sky again, we got word that the choppers were taking us to a village that is supposed to be friendly. At the same time it has *also* been known to draw suspicion.

We ventured towards the area where we would be picked up, and it was highly apparent that all of the rice paddies were flooded. All we could do was walk on the dykes. After the choppers landed, the force of air from their propellers blew me right into the paddy. I found myself quickly sinking into the mud.

First my knees, then to my waist, and then to my chest. At that point I am more scared than I had ever been in Nam. Suddenly, I feel hands going under my armpits, and I was being pulled out by my two heroes, Gator and Indy. Indy is laughing his ass off since I am completely covered in mud. Once I boarded the chopper one of the other soldiers said, "Hey, Short Round, I didn't know they had tunnels on the rice paddies." I felt like a fool.

Once we all landed and secured our location, Top and the Old Man were still laughing their butts off as if they just saw the funniest show on Earth. Sgt. Pete couldn't stop smiling. Meanwhile, I could hardly walk since I was covered in wet mud. Lucky for me, it wasn't but an hour later when a chopper came out with more supplies. Although I had a fatigue shirt and socks in my backpack, I didn't have any extra pants, and my boots were soaked.

Actually, in the new supply cache was a complete wardrobe for almost everyone. That's what I call great timing. Most of us got new uniforms, but only a few of us took new boots. *Man, did I ever feel better*. Armed with another new arsenal of rain to clean us down, and brand new clothes to put on, we were all feeling extremely refreshed, especially me after my own personal mud bath.

After donning our new clothes, securing our camp, and Indy and Gator letting me have their laughter most of the evening, it was time for some shut eye. But not for long, because it was up to Gator and me to pull guard duty. Gator continued to snicker every time he looked at me, thinking of my ever-sinking body into what seemed like the equivalent of quicksand.

Later, once guard duty was over with, we fell asleep in the confines of our hooch. All of a sudden, blood curdling screams start coming from Gator's side. Indy and I both reach for our flashlights. *Oh my God.* A rat the size of a baby possum is chewing on his lip. He's holding it with both hands, trying to pry it off. I reached for my bayonet and started stabbing it. Finally, it releases its bite and scurries off. By that time, half the platoon is at our place.

"Medic, Medic!" I heard Sgt. Pete cry out.

Four medics arrive and bring out a load of bandages. They covered his face. Man, this is gut-wrenching. Wow. Even though it's still dark a chopper is landing already to pick him up. *They certainly get here fast.* Indy and I are holding his hands as he is being rolled on a gurney towards the chopper. You could tell in his eyes that he was scared. In a mere second he was lifted onto the chopper, and away he went.

Oh man, this really hurts. The days dragged on, and it was fairly obvious that Indy and I weren't the same without our third companion. We had no word on Gator for days, but then one morning Top and the Old Man gathered the company and told us that they had some great news.

First, Gator is stateside and is going to be alright. He's going to need some surgery on his face, but he *is* okay. What a relief *that* was to hear. Secondly, in about three days we will be going to Phu Cat, an air force base, to watch the Bob Hope show.

The Old Man looked me in the eyes and said, “We obtained a lot of useful documents a short time ago, and this is our reward.”

We were all jumping up and down with joy. It was hard to contain our excitement, but eventually we knew we had to. Before we left we had some more business to do, so we knew we weren’t out of the woods. *Not yet.*

The Replacement

During this time we started to talk about what we could possibly expect when we saw the show. To us, at this point, *anything* different would be good. I mean, really. Up until this time it was short bouts of action that put our lives at risk every time, followed by long periods of waiting in the equivalent of a mosquito-infested swamp with monsoon-like rains. So we were definitely ready for something different but, alas, we still had a couple of days to wait. It was torture.

With the lack of Gator by our side, Indy and I started walking with Bill and Oreo. It was a great friendship that was developing between the four of us. But no matter how buddy buddy we all were, everyone was all business when we were out walking in the jungle. As a side note, Burns, our new point man, was doing a terrific job.

Overall, I was extremely thankful that I was put in this company. However, as happy of a family as we all seemed to be, like with many circles we have throughout the course of our lives, Vietnam wasn't really that much different. Although I knew almost everyone, we still pretty much had our own little circle of friends, and most of us stayed confined to that circle. It was like what you saw in high school all over again, but without the hidden animosity towards groups that weren't your own. Everyone accepted everyone here, and it's something I don't ever recall seeing prior to being shipped off to this foreign land.

Strong friendships *had* to develop, really, and external acceptance of those who weren't in our own personal circle was a key foundation in keeping our company together. After all, most time in Vietnam was spent waiting on an enemy that we could hardly ever find, so we had to feel like we were a part of something solid in order to keep sane. So although we waited and waited and searched and searched, we always kept our bonds. We were bored to tears, talking until the cows came home, or fighting for our lives. That was Vietnam.

Speaking of randomness, just when the redundancy of nothingness had seemingly caused our brains to melt, it was time for another new adventure. *As always.*

After the last two days had moved like sap dripping down a pine tree, we made a new camp alongside a large hilltop that was very dense with foliage. We had just secured our location when a couple of guys came back from relieving themselves with a bowel movement. Unbeknownst to most civilians, whenever *we* had to go, we had to walk about 25 yards or so with a roll of toilet paper, a shovel, and two others to stand guard. It wasn't the most comfortable thing, and was pretty embarrassing, but that was standard operating procedure. You basically dug a hole about a foot deep, did your business, and then covered it up to hide your tracks.

It seems simple enough, but this time, after these two soldiers returned, I noticed that they went straight to Top, our first Sergeant. Ten minutes later, he told the third platoon to saddle up. Then he looked my direction and said, "Oh, Short Round, you need to come as well, and bring your 45 and a flashlight and leave the rest behind." Great. I know what *that* means. They must have found more tunnels.

As we made our way towards our destination, sure enough, there were several spider holes. I'm thinking that they were empty, because we hadn't seen any movement in the area at all. But you never really know what is down there in that darkness.

Once I jumped down one of the holes, I proceeded my way into one of the myriad number of tunnels. It was very tight going into this one. Like a male porn star making love to a virgin tight. I'm *really* having trouble crawling here. Just then I heard a cough, so I'm really glad I hadn't turned on my flashlight yet. It sounded like the noise was coming from the left, so I attempted to crawl in that direction, which was a little easier now since I was finally able to crawl on my hands and knees.

Suddenly, I hear another cough as I approach a left turn. I can see the glare from his lantern. As I stopped and listened carefully, I could have sworn this guy was talking to himself. After a deep breath, I turned and pointed my weapon in that direction as I ventured around the bend.

Holy shit, there are two of them again. I shoot the first one in the head, and then the other takes off. I missed. The light from my flashlight is sporadically moving in a fashion that would drive most cats crazy as I try to locate him, but it's obvious he's gone. *Where in the hell did he go?* I sure wasn't going to chase him, because then I would no longer have an element of surprise in the equation, and that's what I thrived on.

I'm backing out of this one, and with extreme caution. Luckily, I arrived outdoors without a scratch. Well, sort of. Even though Top is talking to me, I don't hear a single word. Again, my ears are all jacked up.

With ears still ringing, I told him that there were *quite* a few more tunnels down there, but that was all I was doing for the day. I think knowing that someone got away who could possibly be telling others to be on the lookout made me a lot more hesitant to be brave. In my head I pictured all of these hidden soldiers intentionally setting booby traps knowing the U.S. Army was above ground looking for them.

Although Top understood that I didn't want to go down again, at the same time he was also concerned. Once my ears were finally cleared up, I heard him ask, "Short round, when are you giving this up? Because it scares me and the Old Man every time you go in there."

"I'll know when the time has reached its limit," I confidently replied. But I wasn't confident, really. Not like I used to be. Knowing that soldier got away made me somewhat fearful of any potential repercussions. For now, however, I just had to get over it.

I did, quickly, like always. *Or so I thought.*

With my mind trying to force itself elsewhere, I left the proximity of the tunnels with the others and got back to the company. Then the choppers arrived and we ate some chow.

Out of nowhere, this young, baby-faced soldier comes up to me and said he wanted to go down in the tunnels. I heard myself saying, "No way in hell, son." It was funny hearing myself call someone that considering I was five foot two and under a hundred pounds. But at this stage in the game I felt like a father figure to those that came in after me.

"Why should you get all the glory?" he asked.

"Son, it's not glory, it's stupidity."

It was strange hearing myself admit to that, but in a way it's true. Honestly, if it weren't for my upbringing, I have no idea why I would continue to do something like this. It was at this time that I thought maybe I *should* get a replacement, just like when I retired from pulling point. Maybe I was finally realizing my own mortality by having these thoughts. Yet, at the same time, I also wanted to protect this kid from this kind of idiocy. But he kept persisting, and no matter how I felt I just couldn't talk him out of it.

Later that night Top comes up to me and tells me that a GI talked to him who must be as nuts as I am. Even then, he agreed to let him try it out. Tomorrow morning we were going to let him go in. Sad, but most certainly true.

Regardless of his foolish choice, it wasn't something I could be too concerned about. Not *that* night. That night we were *all* on edge because we knew a lot of

Cong was in the area. Usually that also meant that underground tunnels were around, and hidden soldiers could easily come out when we least expected it. Better to be safe than sorry, so we put out extra claymores and trip flares.

Tonight, Bill, Oreo and I were all pulling guard together. It seems like we weren't in the foxhole but fifteen minutes when Lifer started her all-too familiar growl. No one ever doubted her because she's proven herself time and time again. The whole company has learned to trust every single instinct she has. She has never failed us, and she is *always* right on the money.

With the hair standing up on her back, I knew it was time to get Indy. I quickly jumped out and went to my hooch.

"Indy. Indy! Get up! Lifer is at it again." Then he jumps right out of the hooch and runs towards the fourth platoon.

Before I even get back to the foxhole, the sky is being lit up with illumination rounds from our mortar platoon. We couldn't believe what we were seeing. They were lying end to end, all crawling on their backs of all things, and their feet were touching the next Charlie right on their head. When they reached our illumination trip wires, they could tell they were there by touching the wire very lightly with the palm of their hands, and then they tapped the next soldier on the head with their foot. These guys were smarter than they looked.

Overall, it looked like there were twenty or thirty Charlies. But man did we *ever* light them up. Some of the guys had a tracer round on every fifth bullet. Tracer rounds are red in color and you can see the line of fire that you are shooting at. Man it was pretty, especially with the mortar platoon dropping down the rounds with rapid fire. And those machine gunners were unbelievable!!

But the next morning during body count we found out that there were only eight fatalities out there. *What? There was a hell of a lot more than that!* While we believed many had escaped, we also felt like some of them may have ventured into the tunnels. I knew exactly what that meant, but *this* time things were going to be different.

Top took me *and* the new guy that wanted to go down so badly to one of the many tunnels. There were *so* many. I tried to talk this new GI out of it, but he wouldn't have any part of it. So I took his weapon, backpack, and his dog tags and gave him my 45 and my flashlight. Down he went into the unknown.

After about ten minutes we hear shots, and it's not from my 45. It sounds like an Ak-47. We are in shock. I felt it was my fault. But then he emerges from the tunnel, shaking uncontrollably, and his left hand was bleeding like crazy. Since he's been shot, Top calls the first platoon medic to tend to his wounds.

He said that he dropped my flashlight when he got hit, but that was the least of my worries since I'll have a new one on the next chopper. Then he informed us that Charlie took off. At this point I wondered how many were down here.

Top wondered, too. He looked directly at me, and I confirmed his glance by saying, "Let's go get them, but not in *this* tunnel."

The new guy that got shot, with an obviously befuddled expression on his face, point blank said, "Oh, man. You're nuts. Never, ever will I do *that* again."

"Hell no. You probably have a million dollar wound, which means you get to go home without being seriously wounded," I replied.

I was trying on a sarcastic brand of humor in order to get my mind off of what was next. Yet again it was time for business. *So much for my replacement*. On the other hand, I was pissed at myself for letting him go in, and told the higher-ups that the kid just wasn't ready.

When it was time to do what I did best, I looked at all of the available tunnels. Then I quickly checked my 45, which I disassembled and had back together in less than two minutes. It was justified, really, because I don't like the idea of someone else using my weapon.

After I eventually found the hole I was going in, I briefly hesitated. Unbeknownst to those around me, I was seriously not liking the fact that a gook was down there letting others know that we were here. With way too many doubts stuffed into my weary brain, I entered the point of no return. I shined my light for about three seconds and then turned it off for about forty-five, all the while continuing to snake my way down the tunnel.

Ten minutes passed before I saw a light, which was quite a ways away. It was time to turn off my own. In complete pitch black darkness I saw his light inching towards me, closer and closer. *If he gets too close, he's bound to spot me*. So I begin to lay flat on my stomach with the side of my head lying on the ground, as still as a corpse. *Is he too blind to see me?*

While lying perfectly still, I noticed his AK-47 that was strapped over his head and hanging by his side. He's only twenty feet away when I decided to jump on my knees and start firing. I shot three times before the third one finally hit him. Lucky for me, he had no chance to get his weapon to fire back. My bullet hit him in the throat and he was gurgling blood. It was time for the kill. **Boom**. Sympathy shot on my part.

As I crawled out of the tunnel, yet again I started second guessing what I was doing. Every time I went down, I became something that just wasn't me. In addition, I also put my own life at risk every single time. I was in constant conflict between wanting to be a brave soldier and wanting to stop all of this madness and live to see another day.

Hooray for Hollywood

When I finally reached the fresh but unbearably hot and humid air, I was informed that a medevac chopper picked up our wounded kid. I told Top I was done for the day, and he said that it was no problem, especially since we had a show to go see.

The choppers picked us up, and it seemed like we were in flight for thirty minutes. We finally landed at Phu Cat, and we were beyond jacked. The Bob Hope show—how cool was that? When we arrived at our destination, we noticed a big stage, but it seemed a million miles away. Seated for many rows were hundreds of Air Force personnel dressed in all of their pretty blue uniforms. You should have seen the look on their faces when they turned around and saw the infantry fully dressed in combat gear, with dirty fatigues that looked like they had never been washed, scruffy beards, and bad ass attitudes due to what we had been through.

We were really far back, but we didn't care because we were really happy to be out of that jungle. After about twenty or thirty minutes, Bob Hope comes out on stage and everyone starts clapping and hollering. Then he lays it all on the line, and to this day what he did made me have more respect and admiration for the man when compared to *any* celebrity who has ever lived.

"You Air Force guys. I love you to death, but the show will not start until you move back and let the army infantry guys be up front."

He knew fully well by the way we looked that we were in the thick of it, and that is why he felt we deserved to see the show closer than any other. Thankfully, there was no animosity from them. They were completely willing to do as Mr. Hope suggested.

So there I was, a combat-stricken young man from the middle of a giant corn field, now in the front row of a show that contained one of the most famous comedians of our time. When the show began, Bob did his usual comedy routine. Then Joey Heatherton came out and did a little dance. Next, the main attraction for me, and most of the others, was Raquel Welch. When she came out on stage the whistling didn't stop for fifteen minutes. This was the second most beautiful woman I had ever seen in my life, with my wife being the first.

Overall, it was like we were in another world, far away from the place that we had to wake up to every day. After an hour and a half it ended, and when we departed, all of the Air Force guys stood up and they all began clapping for us. That meant everything to us. It really did. During this one brief moment, we were all dropped into what seemed like a dreamy fantasy world, but once it was all over with we were quickly put back into the face of reality. Sadly, all of the choppers picked us up and dropped us off into the jungle once again.

The show was over. We had our second of fun, but we were all back in no-man's land. The journey continued, as always. At least the show gave us something to think about and talk about on our long trek, because we must have walked for a full week after that and never once even saw the faintest hint of a village.

During our march to the unknown, our new orders finally arrived. *Something other than walking. It's about freaking time!* The Old Man gathered us around to tell us that we were going to the rear to pull guard for a support unit. Support units are generally small base camps that deal with maintenance, fueling, preparing meals, as well as a variety of other things. We were kind of relieved in a way since walking without any action was getting to be a trifle bit boring.

When we finally arrived, the guys on the base seemed to be extremely relaxed. We noticed how secure the camp was by all the foxholes, and the number of men pulling guard in the middle of the day started to make us all feel pretty secure. Our mission here was to pull guard at night. Meanwhile, we could walk around freely, but we were to meet in the mess hall at 1300 hours.

While exploring, Indy and the fourth platoon decided to check out the mortar platoon while Oreo and I decided to take in the sights. We noticed an extraordinary amount of jeeps, trucks, and helicopters, with mechanics working on all of them. *Hell, they even had outside latrines.*

We started talking to a guy that was burning the human waste in a big barrel. He said he was a honey dipper. That was his job. I think I'll stick with the infantry. Later on that day, after chowing down at the mess hall, our company got situated in a great location. We had bunkers with sandbags everywhere. This place was kind of neat, and so unlike anything that we were used to. Heck, we were told we could even take off our backpacks, shirts, and just enjoy our visit and relax. Indy, Bill, Oreo, and I spent a lot of time together those next few days, and we could tell it was going to be a friendship that would last forever.

After four days passed, we watched some choppers coming in for fuel, and then we noticed some new recruits getting out. Several hours later, Sgt. Pete gathered the second platoon together and introduced us to a second Lieutenant that would be our new platoon leader. After that Sgt. Pete takes off. As soon as he left this little piece of stateside crap starts barking off orders like we were in basic training. He wanted everyone to salute him. Half the platoon laughed at his obviously uninformed ass. Saluting anyone out here was just asking for them to be shot by a sniper out in the sticks.

Then, he *really* hit a nerve. His orders were that, when we are in the field, we will have an inspection of gear and personal items in our backpack.

"Everything will be clean," he stated.

We all roared so hard some of us started to cry. Someone yelled out for him to write a letter to his family and tell them good-bye, as he wouldn't make it out of the first firefight. He was fuming. When Sgt. Pete came back he instantly sensed the hostility.

After telling our side of the story, Pete took that candy ass youngster to the company Commander. We watched the fireworks in action as the Old Man ripped him a new one. Later that night, the second platoon gathered, and we aired out to this jerk what hell really was. In addition, we informed him that we were all family and that rank meant nothing unless it was the Old Man or Top.

He apologized to us all and started sobbing like a baby. *Oh, crap.* On one hand, I thought he was a wuss. On the other hand, I realize that sometimes people who try to be extremely bossy are actually really fragile inside, and they do that sort of thing to compensate. So, if that was the case, I guess part of me understood. Although, out here, being fragile wasn't something a person could afford to be. I hope we don't have problems with this guy because of it.

Truthfully, it was soon forgotten, especially since more days passed and we were getting pretty darned comfortable. However, nothing in the bush lasts for long. Although it was enjoyable talking to everyone in the company, all good things must come to an end. Before we knew it we were sent back to the field to resume our search and clear missions. After two or three days, it was back in the groove of the same old routine.

As usual, we couldn't find a village to save our souls. Our new point, Burns, was getting discouraged. Then, one day, he found a bit of a clearing and noticed that an army unit had been there previously. So, again, we decided to set up camp.

One day, as I was walking along with Bill, he said that he would see me at chow time because he was off to trim the mortar pit. Thirty seconds later we all hear an explosion that sounded like a monster cannon went off. It felt like an earthquake and came from the fourth platoon. I ran up to the pit to ask Bill what happened, and there he was, lifeless, with no legs and one of his arms gone as well. Bill had just stepped on a 105 artillery round that was a dud, but booby trapped by the Cong.

I was devastated. For days I couldn't function. We came upon several tunnels, but I just couldn't bring myself to go down into any of them. All I could think about was how I made a great new friend and how quickly his life was gone, not to mention the grief that his family would have to endure. It took me a while to get past it, but after several weeks my own personal grief had finally subsided. I *had* to get past it and move on.

Sure, it wasn't easy, but at least something was about to happen to get my mind off of it.

It all started when Burns came back to the company after scouting. He said that he found a village close by. Lucky for us, he said it looked fairly friendly. When we arrived, we noticed a lot of men as well as a few women and children. Little six and seven year old children were pulling on our fatigues asking us if we wanted a dinky dau cigarette for five dollars. That's their term for crazy, otherwise known as marijuana. Others were pulling on our pants, saying boom boom sister, five dollars. Boom boom means having sex. It's pretty sad when kids are selling drugs as well as prostituting out their own family members for cash. As I looked around, I noticed a few GI's pulling out the money for the cigarettes. Although I was a young guy who, of course, was filled with curiosities, I declined.

Feeling the need to explore my surroundings, I continued to walk by the villagers, and I paid close attention to their behavior, which was quite interesting to watch. One was cutting another's hair, and the one getting his hair cut had a huge disfigurement on his face, like it was some kind of burn. The one cutting the hair had a huge scar on his face. Both of these guys were creepy looking, but they were still at least trying to act friendly by holding up one finger and saying, "GI, number one."

Although I tried to smile, it was difficult, because whenever we encountered any men, no matter how friendly they may seem, we always seemed to be attacked soon afterwards. Just then, out of the corner of my eyes, I saw Kit talking to the villagers. Unfortunately, Kit couldn't seem to get any information, but he was content that this was a friendly village. However, after my experiences I knew that was rarely the case.

Later on, we ventured a little past the village and decided to set up camp half a mile away. As expected, that night we were confronted by the Cong. It wasn't much of a battle, and it only lasted about two minutes. The next morning, the body count was three Cong killed, and, sure enough, one was the barber and another was the one that had been getting a haircut.

After seeing this, the Old Man ordered us to go back and burn the village, but to get all the women and children out of there first. When we got there, the whole village was empty. Not one person was in sight. We burned all the huts anyway so they had no chance to return.

Things went by rather slowly after that, as always, but we received some pretty exciting news during this time. As the calendar progressed the rumors started flying like a bat right out of hell. We overheard stories about the Tet Offensive that was going to happen in late January. I guess the Viet Cong and the North Vietnamese armies were going to put forth an all-out effort to overrun major camps occupied by U.S. forces.

Hell, we were so far in the jungle that we never really noticed anything different. January and February passed, and then in March we were sent into Khe Sanh to help support the Marines. We thought it was going to be a hell of a battle, but the confrontation was minimal because the marines had already done a great job. I guess that they had taken major losses, but things seemed to be pretty well in control by the time we got there.

Then it was off to A Shau valley, an area close to the Ho Chi Minh trail, which was a traveling point of the

Cong and the NVA. After two days in the valley, we were in a fire fight that lasted about three hours. We lost sixteen men that day. Only five were dead, but the others were injured so badly that they wouldn't be returning. We were worn out and wanted out of that valley. *Badly.*

It would have been nice, but we weren't able to get out of the woods quite yet. As a matter of fact, Burns came to us during our long walk to recovery and said he found some more tunnels. It had been a while for me, but for some stupid reason I was eager for the games to begin.

I did my ritual of giving my stuff to someone, and down I went. As I shined my flashlight around, all I could see were wires going everywhere. Booby trapped, so I backed out immediately. Then into another one I crawled. It seemed to weave every which way. T intersections, curves, you name it. The damn thing just seemed to go on forever. It was, literally, like an underground city.

As I was just about to give up hope, I saw a huge light. As I approached closer and closer, I noticed that it wasn't a lantern, but a gigantic fire, almost like an underground bonfire. Near it I see two figures, but they're not wearing Viet Cong attire but, rather, NVA uniforms. They had their backs to me as I inched ever-so closer.

They were passing their dinky dau cigarette back and forth while laughing like little school children who were racing home after being at school all day. As I moved within five feet of them, I shoot one in the back of the head. The other reaches for his AK-47, but I hit him dead center in the forehead right as he turns around.

It had been a while, so my adrenaline was really flowing. My ears were ringing like a resonant bell, yet again, from shooting in such a small enclosure. Matching it was my heart, which was pounding like a jackhammer. So I decided to sit next to my prey for a second to calm down.

Just as I'm getting ready to head back to my company I noticed packs of the dinky dau cigs lying next to the bodies. ***Man*** was I curious. Sure, I had smoked maybe one or two stateside, but everyone said these were ten times more powerful. Seeing as how I couldn't take the temptation anymore, I lit one up from the fire.

Holy crap. I inhaled once, and that was, hands down, the most powerful thing in the world. That was it for me. I threw the rest in the fire. It was obvious that one more drag on that cigarette and I probably wouldn't have made it out of these tunnels alive.

Once I was finally out in the open, I told Top that was all I could handle today. Two kills were enough. He just shook his head.

"Get ready. Choppers are on their way," he announced. *Finally.* We're getting the hell out of this God-forsaken valley and dropped back into the more familiar terrain of the jungle. Believe it or not I felt more at home there.

Yet, even though I was headed towards a more comfortable environment, or so I thought, something was on my mind that was truly bugging me. Every day guys were derosing out to go home permanently, or on R and R. *Man, when will it be **my** turn?* Well, as luck would have it, after we were picked up a rumor was circulating that we were going to Da Nang for an in-country R and R. *Finally. Some much needed rest.*

After an hour or so we land and, to our dismay, it isn't Da Nang but, instead, Dong Ha. This is the continuation of where my story originally began.

May 12th, 1968: The Conclusion

Oh my god. Every inch that I crawl backwards I see another American casualty. The wounded and dead are everywhere.

"Short Round, get your ass over here," I heard Top yelling from about ten feet away. There are seven dead bodies around him, protecting him from enemy fire. He is on the horn calling in airstrikes and helicopter fire power. I look him straight in the eyes and the tears are flowing, and then I looked over to see Lifer licking the face of a lifeless body. It's the Old Man, our company Commander.

Out of nowhere I heard, "Short Round. You ok?" It was so good to hear that high, squeaky voice. Indy was alive.

"Yeah. Have you seen Oreo?" I asked.

“He was okay five minutes ago,” he replied. All of a sudden, someone is pulling on my ankle.

“Hey, Short Round, you’re not getting rid of me that quickly,” Oreo whispers.

So here we are. Indy, Oreo, Top, Lifer and I, with bodies everywhere, including the one of our esteemed patriarch. We all huddled together closely, surrounded by a circular stream of our bullets, and hanging on for our very lives.

After an hour of non-stop hell, the airstrikes had made their presence known, and the dunes and everyone in them were finally destroyed. I can just imagine the number of bodies that were buried along with their destruction. But that was not the concern of me or my fellow men. For us, it was our company. We found out later that, after the total count, out of 240 men in our company only forty-seven of us walked out without a scratch. The rest were dead or seriously wounded.

It was a hellacious, sorrowful mess, but at least cleaning it up seemed to go like clockwork. Other units came over to help, and one helicopter after the next picked up our wounded and our dead.

As this was all happening, a moment of intense clarity happened for me as I looked around at the ones that survived this moment in hell. Top stood there, with Lifer in his arms. I, Indy, and Oreo sat together, clasping one another’s hands, probably to stop each other from shaking. All the while knowing how damn lucky we all were to still be alive.

Suddenly, another familiar face joins us. It was Burns. He said that God was looking after his sorry ass, because for some crazy reason the two point men that died begged him to take his place today. Yes, it was definitely his lucky day. It was lucky for ***all*** of us who managed to escape death.

A Break Before Babysitting

After the cleanup continued, Top gathered what was left of us and said we were going to another support base to spend several days there. We needed many more troops due to the number we just lost.

When we arrived at the base camp we were told to chill out for a few days. Heck, we weren't even going to pull guard duty. *How great is that?* However, even though we did feel relaxed due to our new environment and our lack of duties, we were still on edge. At this time we still had no idea who all had lived and who had died. The Old Man, the best friend of everyone, was gone. That we knew, and it was so sad. He had three daughters and a wife. It was *so* tragic.

As I started to feel utterly depressed, Sergeant Pete approached us to lift my spirits. ***Yes!*** My mentor *and* my Idol made it. He proceeded to tell us that the second and third platoon leaders didn't make it. Although my new platoon leader was an ass at first, he came around to our way of thinking. But, unfortunately, he still didn't make it. Sad, but true.

At this time, Sergeant Pete wanted to talk to me personally. He pulled me over to the side and tells me that I just made Sergeant E-5.

"What?!?!?" I gasped.

"Yeah. You're the only one in your actual *squad* to survive, so you get a field commission to non-commissioned officer of E-5. Your paperwork is going in tonight," he announced. Wow. Sergeant by default. Who knew *that* would ever happen?

Then I was informed that since we're going to be here a while that I, as well as a few others, were being sent on R and R.

When I was asked where I wanted to go, I said, "Hawaii. I want to go to Hawaii."

After about a week everything was in order, but then Top walked up to me with a telegram from the Red Cross, telling me that I was the proud daddy of a baby boy who was born on the sixth of that month. Oh man, the world just got better. But then it hit me. Although I was smiling from ear to ear knowing I was a father, I knew I'd have to wait a while for my trip because of my wife just giving birth. Top understood, and reassured me that we were staying put for a long time.

Most of those who were eligible were already back from their R and R before I left. Then, finally, it was my turn. Oh, man, it was *such* a great feeling that I instantly found out why so many went AWOL (Absent without leave).

My wife was *so* excited to see me when we met at the Honolulu airport. When I first spotted her as I made my way off the plane she was, truly, what I thought was the most beautiful sight in the world. I had a whole week with the love of my life. Sadly, since he was so young my baby boy couldn't accompany her and was being watched by my mother-in-law. But my wife showed me pictures of our new baby, and I truly couldn't wait to meet him.

One day, I thought. *One day*. In the meantime, I intended to spend every waking second with my bride. While my love and I were in Hawaii, we walked on the beach, of course, and we even went to see Don Ho and his Tiny Bubbles show. But most of the time it was *quality time* spent with the love of my life.

Overall, the week seemed like only one day since time stopped when I was with her. Before I knew it I had to return to my unit. On the plane, I was hoping like mad that this wasn't my last time to be stateside in an upward position. I wanted to return to her. I also wanted to meet ***him***. I *had* to.

When I arrived back at my company, I was greeted by the cheers of my fellow soldiers. *Wow, did they miss me that much?* As expected, we were still at the same support base camp. I asked what was going on, and they said we just had some sniper fire every once in a while, but that was pretty much it. It seems as though Top, a couple of Louies, and Sgt. Pete would be running the show.

A couple of days passed, and we all awaited the abundance of new recruits that were supposed to enter our unit. All greenhorns, fresh out of boot camp. *Great.* I was not looking forward to playing babysitter for what would now be three fourths of our company. But I guess I had no choice.

When the day arrived I never recalled seeing so many helicopters in the sky. As I watched them land I found it rather funny considering all that I've been through. They were jumping out, all slouched over like we were in full combat.

While I'm watching this, Indy pokes me and asks, "Remember those days when you started?"

"Yeah, I was scared shitless," I replied.

"Well, so are they," he reminded me. Being out here so long, I guess it's really easy to forget.

Three choppers were left to land, and then the most bizarre thing happened. I see Elvis, yet again, shaking hands with the heavy set guy that got shot in the leg when he jumped off a chopper to come to our company several months ago. Just like before, an AK-47 open fires from off in the distance. This guy truly has *no* luck.

We see the culprit and all start unloading on the sniper immediately. The heavy set guy is bleeding from the arm, and then once again Elvis pulled his unlucky ass back into the chopper. *Are you kidding me*? What are the odds of *that*? It was truly unreal. I guess the Cong instinctively seeks out the bigger targets. Good thing I'm not one of them.

Once the sniper is confirmed as being dead, Top brings me nine greenhorns.

"Short Round, these guys are all yours," he says.

I replied instantly with a heart-felt plea. "But Top, why don't you give me a couple of the old timers and the rest greenhorns?"

"Can't do that, Sarge," he replied. *Sarge. I loved the sound of that.* "Don't worry, you aren't the only one getting all new guys," Top explains.

I suppose that appeased me, but it still seemed like a lot of responsibility so soon. However, if there's anything I learned out here, it's that you learn to swim by being thrown into the water, not adjusting to the temperature and walking through the shallow end first.

So here I am, a literal youngster myself, but surrounded by a bunch of new, freshly shaven faces, all sitting around me like little schoolchildren taking in a story at bedtime. Since it was story time, I decided to start with the basics.

"First thing's first. You will all eventually have a nickname. You will not bunch up when we see action. Watch from me and learn, but if you really want to learn, watch our platoon sergeant, Sgt. Pete. He's the best."

I then proceeded to tell them that it is always miserably hot, so they need to get used to it. In addition, I stressed that they should never go down in the tunnels because we already have an idiot who does that. *Yours truly.*

It was also emphasized over and over again that they needed to stay focused at all times. After that I spent the rest of the day showing them how to make a hooch. Finally, I helped to get all of their supplies ready so they were all equipped for battle. But seriously, were they *really* ready? I guess the only way to find out was once a firefight began.

Overall, when I looked at these kids, I could tell by the look on their faces that they had the same, unusually strange juvenile mix of fear and curiosity that I had when I first arrived. It was a look that, unfortunately, I'm betting I still had from time to time. At that moment, it quickly became all too clear to me that youth often equals curious foolishness.

Since I was the new king of their castle I needed to set a better example for them than I set for myself. All I could really do was try to lead them away from that curious nature, and find a way to protect their lives. I was responsible for them, and I didn't take that responsibility lightly.

A couple of days later we departed for the jungles again, but with a brand new entourage. For some of us it was for the hundredth time, but for the new recruits it was for the very first time, right smack dab in the middle of a whole new world. I was shaking, literally, because these new guys hadn't even fired a round, and I really didn't know what to expect.

In addition, it was our first day in the field in a long time. At first it seemed peaceful. We stopped for lunch and were all casually walking around. Everything seemed okay. All of a sudden we hear the sound of an AK-47, and two of our greenhorns drop.

A Cong runs like the wind on the rice paddy docks with his weapon at his side, and then the whole company unloads their weapons on him. He drops, face down. Taking extreme caution as we approach him, we make sure that he is alone. *He is*. As we turn him over, we're in shock. I'll be damned, it was a female. She was dead and bleeding like a stuck hog, and I think everyone in the company got a direct hit on this one. But she deserved it. After all, she just killed one of the greenhorns and seriously wounded the other. Man, this is getting old. I'm tired of seeing people get shipped off in body bags.

Admirable, but Nuts

A few more days go by, and just like that the weather turns cool out of nowhere, and then the rains become so heavy that we can't even see. Top said we are now in the monsoon season, so this is weather we need to expect. Oreo, Indy and I were stuck in our hooch for days. Even though we were in the deepest part of the jungle, it was so utterly wet that we felt like we were going to get washed away at any moment. To make matters worse there was guard duty. Pure, unadulterated hell since it was nothing but mud we were standing in while being drenched for hours on end by the cold, endless rain.

The only good thing about this time was mail call. Many of us received care packages of goodies, and my mother had sent me sausages and crackers and tons of candy. Indy and I ate some food out of the c-ration cans and then turned them upside down and put heating tabs underneath them. After that, we would then fry pieces of sausage. Everyone was coming to our hooch wondering where that great smell was coming from. That was pretty much the high point during this horrible weather.

After all, it was downright frigid for us since the temperature dropped down to the 50's, which was quite extreme since we were used to 115. But we survived. The rains hit us with all they had, and then the sun finally came out and warmed everything back up again with a vengeance. Once the heat and humidity kicked in, we were all in our own personal sauna once again.

After that the journey continued, and Burns led us to more villages, which didn't pan out to be much of anything. One of the more exciting things to happen at this time was when we were out in the open and a water buffalo charged us. *Now that is frightful.* Those things can get enormous with a capital E, and it took three clips from someone in the first platoon to bring him down.

In a strange way it proved to me more than anything that we were definitely not at the top of our chain. If it weren't for guns, no matter how big or ferocious we humans think we are, there's always going to be some creature bigger or more ferocious. Lucky for us, we were in Vietnam and not Africa. Therefore, water buffalo was about the scariest thing you could find. Everything else that you should be in fear of walked on two legs, carried a gun, and wore black pajamas.

As we creeped along the woods as carefully as ever, many days passed without even the slightest hint of action after that water buffalo incident. However, as always, we knew that was something that could quickly change. *It did.*

One day, when we started walking along the tree line, we decided to cross a rice paddy. All of a sudden we started getting mortar fire from about three hundred yards away. It seemed like a lost cause returning fire because they were hidden extremely well.

Unfortunately, Top told us that the choppers couldn't get to us for over an hour since they were on a mission with another company. The funny thing is that, via binoculars, we noticed that their mortar crew only had a total of three Cong. Yet they still had our whole company pinned down. They were *that* good.

Out of nowhere, I heard, "Short Round, let's go." It was Sergeant Pete.

"Go where?" I asked.

"You and I are going to take them out," he replied.

"What's this we shit, Sarge?" I yelled back. He then proceeded to state his case.

"Hey, look, I've been in the army a long time, and you're the bravest little shit I've ever seen."

"Sorry, Sarge. Not volunteering for this one," I firmly announced.

"Okay. You'll be sorry you missed out," he replied.

At that moment, I didn't know what I was more in shock of. The fact that Sgt. Pete wanted to take these guys out alone, or the fact that I finally declined a suicide mission. Maybe I was finally starting to protect my own butt, realizing my own mortality. Perhaps you can only do so many dangerous things before you finally start to grow up and realize you only have one life to live.

Regardless of these thoughts, apparently they were of no consequence to Sgt. Pete. He took off anyway. In forty-five minutes we see a figure of a man, via binoculars, walking up behind the three in the hole. *What the hell is he doing?*

He lays down his M16, pulls out his bayonet knife, jumps in the hole, and stabs all three until they are dead. *Holy shit*. Although I admired him as a great soldier, I have to admit that move was a bit psychotic. When he returned, he had a big old smile planted smack dab on his face.

He looks at me and says, "Short Round, you missed all the fun."

"It didn't look like a good time to me," I reply.

Overall, this guy made my bravery, or stupidity depending on how you looked at it, seem pale in comparison. At least when I went down in the tunnels I never knew what to expect. Yet he knew ahead of time he'd have to take out three of the enemy. Even then, he dropped his gun and used a ***knife*** because it was more challenging for him.

I never really could figure out why he'd take such a gamble. Was he looking for a medal? Did he want to get killed for some reason? Did he just want to have one last hurrah before he went back home? I seriously didn't know. All I knew was that as time went on Sgt. Pete started to act differently. He was overly quiet, and seemed to shake and act quite nervous. I talked to Top about it, and he said that Pete was going home in two weeks. Top said he was going to make sure he got there, so he was sending him to the rear.

After two weeks were up and it was finally time for him to depart, Pete gave me a hug and told me he wished I was his son. *Wow. What a compliment.*

Overall, everyone was extremely sad to see the master leave, but he put in his time so we were also happy for him. When it came time for him to go, he boarded the chopper and off he went. The legend was now gone, and just like when the Old Man passed away, we never felt the same again.

With a large part of our armor now missing, we all felt the chink of the absent piece, but we knew we had to move on. We drudgingly continued, and had many more search and clear missions, but none of them really amounted to a hill of beans. Until one day we hit the jackpot. Tunnels everywhere, but no sign of Charlie. However, as we found out during past missions, that often meant squat.

So, yet again, I started preparing myself to go down one of the tunnels, but this time when I looked down Lifer was right by my side.

"No, sweetheart, you can't go," I said.

"Aw, let her go," Top requested. I wasn't totally comfortable with the situation, but I thought, hey, why not?

As we ventured down the rabbit hole, with her walking in front of me, I noticed it was a monstrous complex. Individualized rooms everywhere, but not one sign of another human being.

After about fifteen minutes or so, I hear Lifer growling. I start getting scared, thinking she will give away my location, or at least make the Cong come running because they thought they just heard dinner. While watching the hair rise on her back, I see her slow prance quickly come to an abrupt halt as she stops dead in her tracks.

All of a sudden she takes off running, and then I see a flash from two feet away. A Cong soldier was straight ahead, and he was shooting at the dog. I pointed and pulled my trigger and then heard the all-too-familiar thud once his body hit the ground.

First I shined my light on him to make sure he was really a goner. *He was*. Dead as a doornail. *But where is Lifer?* I'm shining my light left and right, and all of a sudden she puts her front paws on my leg. I see her, wagging her tail as always. I am ***so*** thankful that he missed our mascot. *What a dog.*

We both emerged from the hole. Top was right there, waiting for us.

"We found several tunnels over here, Short Round," he exclaimed.

Sure, why not, I thought to myself. Without saying a word, I proceeded to go down another, but without Lifer this time. I'm only one hundred feet into the tunnel when I see a light, so I turned my flashlight off for good.

As I inch closer and closer, I noticed that this tunnel had turns absolutely everywhere. It was time to make my move, so when I turned and was a mere two feet from the light I started to pull the trigger.

But no one was there. *What the hell? Where is he?*

I turned around and instantly felt the end of his AK-47 against my forehead. My life flashed before me. All I pictured at that split second was a sobbing wife home alone with a newborn who was not able to comprehend why his mother was so sad.

My eyes briefly looked at the man in uniform, and it was instantly obvious that he was of the NVA. No wonder he got the drop on me. They were much better trained than the Cong.

His eyes were black as coal, and he started smiling a rotten tooth smile and then said something that I obviously couldn't understand. To this day, I would love to know what it was. If only I could remember so someone could translate it for me.

Yet, at the time, it didn't really matter what he was saying to me. All I knew was that any memory of words would be short-lived. I was in a nightmarish dream that I was never going to wake up from. Surprisingly, I heard the click from his gun, but I was still here.

His weapon had jammed, and then as if by mere instinct four shots rang out from my 45. I'm absolutely shaking, and as I walked back to the serenity of daylight I was sweating so much that my uniform looked like I had just swam a few laps in one of the deeper canals.

Top looks at me, with a look of fright that I never recalled seeing from him, and said, "Oh my god, you're as white as a sheet."

My quick response was simply, "I'm done, Top. No more. Ever again. I'm done."

"You never should have started, son," he replies with a half-cocked smile and a tilted head. With his smile still firmly in place he quickly nods in utter agreement to my *finally* grown-up words.

Farewell: The Bamboo Bye-Bye

After a few more days passed, I sat down and discussed the prospect of going home with Top. I was ready. *It was time*. As we were discussing my departure, I mentioned that he was here before me, yet *I* only had a few weeks left. More than anything I was curious why he was still here. He told me that he had re-upped his duty a couple of months ago.

"Besides, someone has to take care of Lifer, and one of these months we'll get a new Old Man," he affirms.

Unlike Top, I had become quite aware that I no longer had any motivation to be here. Not only because of the horrors of war. Or because my youthful exuberance had finally made me value my life even more. But, rather, because the family I had made here was slowing dissipating.

Indy had gone home, and it was only me and Oreo. Burns was at his best, and he and Oreo were getting along pretty well, so I knew they would both be in good hands. Everyone, and I mean everyone, knew it was my turn to part ways.

Wow, what a ride it's been. From small town boy to fighting for my life and the life of others each and every single day. It was a journey, and one I truly don't know if I should remember or purposefully forget.

Overall, when the realization hit me that it was time to go, it became abundantly clear that everyone must have respected me. Mainly because the amount of well-wishing I received as I prepared to go back home was astonishing. Everyone in the whole company was shaking my hand and patting me on the back as I boarded the chopper. The deafening blades made their presence known to me for what would be one of the last times.

Oreo and I exchanged addresses and phone numbers, and I told him to be careful because he only had two months to go. I was losing a few remaining friends due to parting, but at the same time, man, it truly felt great to go home. It was like the whole world had been lifted off my shoulders, and I felt like I was finally close enough to reach the stars.

But before I went home, they were taking me to Cam Ranh Bay in order to get processed. Cam Ranh is a very secure location and supposedly a great place. When I arrived, I quickly understood how much of an understatement that actually was. Showers, towels, clean uniforms, clean mess halls, and large tents with cots. *How do you get **this** gig?*

As I was walked around, I noticed a couple of bars, and outside were posters of Asian groups that would sing there at night. It's amazing how the other half lives. While I was fighting for my life, other soldiers got to have nightly entertainment.

After I did all of my processing to leave the country, I had two days left before I was going to leave. Since I had nothing better to do, I decided to go and have a beer in one of the bars. Once I sat down, out comes the bartender. *Holy crap. He looks just like the guy that stepped off the chopper twice and got shot both times. He really does.*

Just to prove a hunch, I asked him how he got his job.

"You have to get shot twice in the matter of seconds," he replied.

"Were you supposed to be with the 1st Cav?" I asked.

"Yep. 2nd of the 5th," he responded yet again.

"Hot damn. I saw you get shot both times."

My suspicions were confirmed. It *was* him. He was ecstatic that I recognized who he was, and we were both amazed at how wild it is that we were both in the same place at this particular moment in time. We talked for hours, and he said he was very fortunate not to get hurt worse *or* end up being in our company.

"You guys went through hell," he remarked.

After a while of babbling, he said he wanted to introduce me to someone, who also happens to be his boss.

"He's in the back room. Let me go get him."

A couple of minutes later he walks out with none other than Elvis. He just ran to me and bawled like a baby.

"You ignorant ass, what the hell were you thinking? I heard all that you did back there," he remarked.

"Balls bigger than my brains," I jokingly replied.

After a few short chuckles, the three of us talked for a couple of hours. I learned that Elvis re-upped since they promised him the job as night club boss. Soon after that the crowds started pouring in so we cut it short by saying our goodbyes.

Seeing him was fitting, really. He was one of the first people I saw in this country, and he'll also be one of the last.

Finally, my time there was done. I was on my way home and on to the freedom bird. *Well, not quite*. Once I got to the states, I still had six months left in the army. The big difference is that I would eventually be in some cushy stateside location as opposed to out in the middle of the jungle getting shot at every day.

The trip there was lengthy. First a stop in Guam, and then Portland. From Portland to Chicago. Great flights, really, although way too long.

As one would expect, the closer I got to home the more elated I felt. Then, finally, Chicago to Decatur on an Ozark. I was scared shitless since it rattled all the way home, but I was finally there.

I met up with my wife and parents, and for the first time I looked into the eyes of my new baby boy. Without a doubt I realized all of the special things that I was truly risking when I was overseas.

After a few weeks went by, my wife, new baby boy and I had to make our way to my final destination with the Army, which was in Fort Gordon, Georgia.

What the hell? That was a Military Police and Signal Depot installation, so I couldn't really figure out why they were sending me there. Regardless of that fact, we quickly settled in, and found a trailer off base with our new son.

During the first day of formation, there were a total of fifteen of us. Myself and another Sergeant, four spec 4's, and the rest PFC's (Private first class). I and the other Sergeant were assigned to the supply unit. A warrant officer was in charge and said he had nothing for us to do. Nothing major, that is.

Every morning we were to spend all day in Augusta and bring back a packet of screws or a whisk broom just to get us out of his hair. It was easy breezy, and I know it was our reward for being in battle. However, without warning the base Commander chimed in and decided we were going to start up a group that would put on demonstrations for riot control. Then we'd present them to dignitaries. Naturally, us Vietnam vets were elected.

It was a great thought, in theory, but four a.m. formations, practicing all day and putting on the demos at seven at night weren't things we were looking forward to. We deserved better than this after all that we did for our country. I got fed up, rounded all fifteen of us up, and we marched our little asses down to the Inspecting General. He had no idea we were putting in so many hours, so he quickly canceled the program. Afterwards, he said he wanted to talk to each of us on an individual basis.

Once my name came up, he stated, "I see in your files that you've been awarded many honors, with the bronze star for valor, and clusters to go with it. In addition, you got the combat infantry badge and the air medal." Knowing he was getting at something, I knew I had to see what he was getting *at*.

"What do you want, sir? Because those things don't mean crap to me."

"I'm willing to give you $10,000 to re-up," he firmly replied. I responded to his offer as kindly as I could.

"Sir, with all due respect, the army can kiss my ass. The answer is no."

Shocked, but still holding a firm gaze, he said, "Well, the others said the same thing, but they were a little kinder with their reply."

But I didn't care. Sending a young man who was constantly trying to prove himself and be brave into another deathly game of life roulette wasn't something I would care to repeat. I did my time, I served my country, and I learned my lessons well.

I got out of the army with pride and honor to have served my country, but at the same time completely woke up to the harsh realities of what I had risked. Sure, my beautiful family saw me leave as a boy and return as a man, and, for that, part of me feels like I should be thankful. But is growing up really risking your life repeatedly like I did?

The more time goes on, the more I feel as though growing up isn't about bravery, being tough, or taking unnecessary risks. Growing up is realizing that what you have at home is worth protecting your butt over, and that you should avoid such haphazard paths at all costs and just worry about protecting yourself in order to keep your family intact.

This wasn't something I learned until later in life, long after I left the echoes of war far behind me. Perhaps this is why the army prefers to recruit younger men, because they realize many are out to prove themselves and haven't had a chance yet to realize what's really important.

As for me, I got lucky. I really did. Although I was brave and foolish all at the same time and still made it through without a hitch, many who tried to do the same thing came home in body bags, never to see their families again.

Overall, maybe the reason I was willing to take such risks was because my friends that I made in Vietnam were like another family to me. Perhaps I figured the more risks I took, the more I could keep them safe. I really don't know. To this day, I am still torn as to who I should have been protecting. My new friends overseas, or myself so that I had a greater chance to return to my family safe and sound.

Although I don't always think about these things, when I do it becomes obvious that recollecting and having a sense of clarity can sometimes be beneficial. *Sometimes.*

You can actually learn some pretty valuable things that way which you can take with you on your journey through life. So what did I learn? It's simple, really. I learned that with each bad thing that happened to me, something about that happening was extremely good.

Starting off early in life, I realized that divorced parents can crush a child, but if two people weren't meant to last due to one person or another, then sometimes it's better that they be set free so that they have a chance to find their own, true happiness.

Later I realized, with my step-father, that sometimes people who may seem to hate us may actually love us and show it in strange ways. My Step-Father always tried to protect me because I was so small, and tried non-stop to form me into a strong man capable of defending myself and instilling a sense of pride in me with what I had.

As I journeyed my way through high school, I realized that true friends and those who have faith in you won't care how big or small you are or even how weird you may seem, but just that you remain true to yourself and who you are deep down inside.

Later on, once high school had finally ended and I began searching for jobs, although I didn't realize this until after I was out of the army, getting passed down for factory work and ending up at the Post Office was actually a Godsend. That job was one of my greatest pleasures in life. I made an abundance of friends and, truthfully, most people on my route became friends to me more than customers. Even when it was bitter cold in the dead of winter, their smiling and friendly faces were always there to comfort me.

Then there's Vietnam. I took a lot of unnecessary risks. It's true. Sure, perhaps I feel I needed to prove myself due to my years of conditioning by my Step-dad. Yet, the more I think about it, the more I realize that I was probably just protecting my new second family.

Over and over a little voice inside of me said, "If you have confidence that you can do this, then you will not only do it, but protect those people you have learned to care about." Truthfully, I did care about the people I was able to know, and to this day I am beginning to believe that had a lot to do with why I did what I did.

The people I came to know while in that chaotic world during that one brief moment in time were numerous, and I remember some pretty great things about many of the guys who fought by my side.

One name I will never forget, of course, is Elvis. He was one of the first people who brought me into that new world, and was one of the last ones I saw on my way out of it. His outgoing demeanor always stood out, and he made me feel like his best friend even from the very beginning.

Two others that will always remain in my thoughts are Gator and Indy. To this day I remember Gator's shy persona, but deep within was an obvious aura of confidence. He also had a heart of gold. Or Indy, my Midwestern neighbor by a state, a likeable guy with an intelligence that was obvious to everyone. Being great at his job was an understatement, and he seriously should have been an Officer.

Of course, then we had the Old Man. Such a great loss. He was everyone's father in a way, and we all looked up to him. He reeked of authority, but it never got to his head, and it was obvious how he was always looking out for everyone in the company. Then there's Top. A bit crusty and scornful around the edges, but a true soldier and leader in every single way.

Sgt. Pete was another name I will never forget. To some, he was a bit nuts. To others, he was fearless. To me, he was a bit of everything, but more than anything he was truly the best soldier I have ever seen. A survivor, a skilled tactician when it came to war tactics, and he had more bravery in his little finger than I had in my entire body. This man was the living embodiment of a warrior in every sense of the word.

Another name that I will always remember is that of Loner. He treated war like a jig-saw puzzle, and carefully analyzed each piece before making his move. Although he was misunderstood by many within our company, he was still extremely respected by everyone who knew him.

As for the only non-human of our group, Lifer the wonder dog quickly became everyone's best friend. She hated the Vietnamese with a passion, probably due to what they did to her family. Due to this, she could sense when any of them were near long before any of *us* could. She saved my life and the life of many in our company countless times, and finding her was one of the best things that ever happened to us.

We also had Burns, Lieutenant Jerry, and Bill. Burns, a great learner who handled my teachings well and showed no fear. Lieutenant Jerry, one of the nicest officers a person could meet. And Bill, although his life was cut short long before his time, was a very nice young man and extremely skilled in demolitions.

One of the last men I encountered during my tour was Oreo. A soft-spoken, super nice guy, he and I talked about anything and everything. He was one of the primary reasons the end of my tour in Nam became tolerable.

Although I encountered many others along the way, my memory isn't as good as it used to be. All I can say is that everyone I encountered, in some way, shape or form, had strengths that were extremely admirable. Whether they ended up going home or never making it out of that hell-hole, I am glad to have had the chance to meet them.

Overall, I learned a great many things throughout the course of my life. Just by my experiences and the people I encountered, especially during war-time, I was transformed into the person I am today. Hopefully by coming across my path I managed to have an influence on them as well. I can only hope.

Whatever the case may be, as I look back at my time spent overseas, I know for a fact that I learned to appreciate freedom and what I had a lot more than I did before I entered the war. In a way, I thought that this had to do with being a bigger man or, in a grander scheme, the bigger country.

I went over there to fight, but I had it all wrong. Fighting for my country, though admirable, wasn't the lesson that I needed to learn to truly feel like I was free. With thoughts of my friends, both current and old, my parents, my newly rediscovered biological father whom I reunited with later on and, of course, my loving wife and my two children, the *real* lesson that I have learned in my life has *always* been about making connections. *That* is what has truly set me free.

I realized that with every last bond you make with someone, it's something that can stick with you forever.

Whether traumatic or wonderful, having both experiences with people are the only ways we can truly ever say that we have lived, and *I* have lived.

I'm not a hero, I'm just someone who has learned some very important lessons in some very unique ways, some great and some unfortunate. The true heroes, in my opinion, are the ones who sacrificed it all and no longer have the means to tell their *own* stories. They are the only ones who *deserve* all the glory. As for the rest of us who were in the field and survived, the truth of the matter is simple, really. We all got lucky, and that's the *only* reason we're still around. It wasn't skill, strength, *or* bravery. Just dumb-ass luck.

Made in the USA
Monee, IL
10 December 2023

48683088R00105